The Story of
LOW GERMAN
& PLAUTDIETSCH

Tracing a Language
Across the Globe

The Story of
LOW GERMAN
& PLAUTDIETSCH

Tracing a Language
Across the Globe

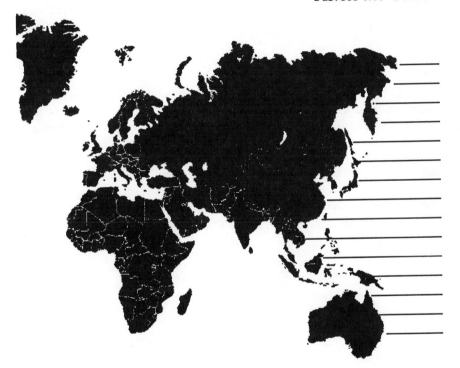

REUBEN EPP

The
Reader's
Press
Hillsboro, Kansas
USA

The Story of Low German—and Plautdietsch

First Edition The Reader's Press

Printed in the USA
by Multi Business Press

ISBN: 0-9638494-0-9

Library of Congress No.: 93-85922

Contents

Maps

Schematics

Foreword

I am often asked by Mennonites who know of my interest in things Mennonite whether I speak Low German. Alas, I have to admit that I do not. But the question is always posed with an air of friendship and hope, while my negative response is greeted with clear disappointment. Somehow, if I but spoke Low German, this would truly make me an "insider"; knowledge of Mennonite life and history is fine, even congregational membership would be a bonus, but to speak Low German . . . then I really would have arrived!

I should perhaps feel flattered that the question is posed at all, for to be asked by a Mennonite of "Russian" descent if you speak Low German is really an invitation to enter a community linked by history and culture, rather than to become a member of a religious denomination. Low German has little to do with Mennonite faith, but it has everything to do with the strong sense of being and belonging that Russian Mennonites and their descendants have developed over a long period. Strangers would rarely be asked this question, because the language is part of a private, inner world of hearth and home, not the public domain of church or town. For this reason, many Mennonites have felt ashamed of speaking Low German in public and in the presence of outsiders. Others have felt that Low German should not be spoken at all as it was far too "earthy", reflecting a language not befitting a Christian people.

Such negative opinions of Low German persist, but happily attitudes in recent years have changed. As Reuben Epp's account clearly shows, Low German should be recognised as a fully-fledged language in its own right, with its own distinctive history, worthy of study by Mennonites as an important part of their heritage. But this recognition has come rather late as in North America at least, use of the language by Mennonites is in rapid decline.

Low German is a language with an honourable past, but with few historical records to chart its origin, connections and importance. To reconstruct the language's past and significance, Reuben Epp has used a wide range of evidence with skill and imagination. Shaped by history, custom and faith the story of the language, recounted here by Reuben Epp, is both fascinating and well told. As he shows, Low German belongs to an ancient and rich tradition of speech and oral culture which ranges across northwestern Europe and includes English, the languages and dialects of the Netherlands and northern Germany and through a massive diaspora, of which Mennonites were a part, once reached into eastern Europe, Russia and Ukraine. Through emigration the language has moved on to North and South America.

The origin of Low German lies in the very beginnings of the development of the Germanic languages. Its golden age in northern Europe, as Reuben Epp shows, is closely connected with the rise and prosperity of the Hansa trading centres. In medieval times this not only created a community of speakers, but also witnessed the development of Low German as a literate language with an emergent literary tradition. But the decline of the Hansa and the rise of High German from the sixteenth century onwards hindered the development of the language in these new directions. While Low German remained an important feature of many speech communities and of oral cultures, it was not until the nineteenth century that it reemerged as a literary language by which time High German, now closely associated with emergent German nationalism, had become dominant. Low German, however, has survived and today is still spoken by over seven million people.

So, across the centuries, in different localities and in varied contexts, Low German has exhibited a remarkable consistency and a spirit of creativity. It is not perhaps surprising that as Mennonite speakers of Low German moved across the vast north European plain, away from the lowland coasts of the Netherlands, through the rivers and forests of northern Germany and the deltas and valleys of Poland and eventually out of the treeline onto the vast, open steppes of Russia and Ukraine, the language helped preserve the essence of community while also proving adaptable to new conditions and environments. In a community with few internal social barriers, in lands without fences or other barriers, language created solidarity while also encouraging adaptation and innovation.

Low German was learnt at mother's breast, in mother's kitchen, sitting at the dinner table, playing in the yard. There were no school teachers or grammars to enforce conformity, no dictionaries to check the "exact" meanings of words. Instead, words and phrases were thrown out without thought of "correctness"; spoken Low German could be fun, harsh, sad and even a little naughty. Comment and conversations, observations and orders, cries and criticism, jest and jeers—the endless repartee of Mennonite life—made Low German a living force.

But all the millions of words Mennonites must have spoken over hundreds of years have mostly been lost: swept away on steppe winds, lost in the prairie vastness, melted in the chaco heat. Only in recent times has the language been studied, only in this century have the words been written down, studied and moulded into a creative literature. Perhaps it is significant that many of those who in recent times have studied Low German, have also created a new literature in the language, combining scholarly study with an obvious love of their mother-tongue: Victor and Elisabeth Peters, Jack Thiessen, Al Reimer and of course, Reuben Epp himself. Hopefully this study will help a wider audience to understand and appreciate Low German and its place in Mennonite history.

Dr. James Urry
Reader in Anthropology
Victoria University of Wellington, New Zealand

Preface

The spawning of my interest in the relationship between Low German and English occurred during a lesson in English literature while in public school. Our class had been assigned the reading of a portion of literature written by Geoffrey Chaucer in the English of his day. After reading it, we were to complete our assignment by translating Chaucer's Middle English into present-day English.

I remember finding it easier to transcribe the Middle English than did my English-only classmates because, as it seemed, the Chaucerian words that I could not recognize in modern English I could easily understand in my Low German mother tongue. At the time, I was baffled and intrigued by this enigma which, for reasons I then could not understand, placed me ahead of my English-speaking classmates in comprehension of Middle English. For the first time, I became aware of an apparent relationship between Low German and the English of Chaucer's writings. I was curious about why so many words were the same in both languages. I do not remember the teacher clarifying this relationship, but I resolved someday to find answers to the questions raised and to satisfy the curiosity awakened by this lesson in English literature.

In later years, as time and resources allowed, I pursued my hobby of exploring the connection between English and Low German. Tracing the story of the English language back to its origins was easy because there was so much information available, dating back to the time of the Anglo-Saxon occupation of Britain fifteen centuries ago. But beyond and aside from that, the background story of the Angles and Saxons seemed more elusive. I could find little, if anything, written in history books about those Angles and Saxons who did not join the occupation of Britain.

Our own Low German people, even those whom I regarded as being educated, generally knew little about the origins of our mother tongue. Back then, that part of their heritage seemed to merit neither their esteem nor their attention. It took decades, it seemed, before I met those few who directed me toward sources of factual information about it.

I learned that the history of Low German is well recorded, but almost entirely in literature printed in Germany. Fortunately, I had by then become quite proficient in reading German. Bit by bit and book by book, I acquired information about Low German in the form of books and documents printed in Germany. Eventually, the Low German literature and scholarly works that I had gathered provided the desired information about the origins of Low German and its ancient connections to English. I could answer most questions about Low German and satisfy my curiosity by turning to the appropriate page.

The compiled information deals with the interrelationships between Low German and English, and where and how the Plautdietsch dialect of the netherlandic Mennonites originated. Since this information has been gathered, it seems appropriate to transcribe a pertinent and interesting condensation of it into English for the benefit of interested North American readers.

Among the few random pieces of information about Low German that had reached me by word of mouth from our own people, some "facts" subsequently proved to be figments, apparently handed down from preceding generations with other folklore, under the guise of historical fact. Unchallenged repetition of such "facts" among succeeding generations, but in the absence of countervailing factual information, seemed to have led to naive acceptance of them as historical truth.

One of the priorities in writing this story of Low German is to acquaint readers with historical truth. Factuality must predominate in a writing which extends and updates what is known about the language. However, insistence upon factuality also risks confrontation with some currently-held misperceptions. Rather than timidly avoiding them, it seems more appropriate to aspire to a dictum expressed by B.H. Unruh in his major research work, here trancribed from his German version on page 82: "In this work the last word is held by scholarly research; not by pretensions, sensitivities nor by petty jealousies."

One of the aims of this story is to provide documented statistics on the numbers of speakers of Low German in various countries around the world. After first adopting this aim, it proved to be difficult, even impossible, to obtain statistics for some countries. For others, figures from various sources were inconsistent.

Instead of letting the scarcity of proven information determine that I omit this important and interesting facet of the story of Low German, I decided to present the reader with figures obtained from seemingly reasonable sources and, where numbers were lacking, to make gap-filling projections. Therefore, it also becomes incumbent upon me to caution readers of possible inaccuracies among quoted statistics on speakers of Low German. I have been careful to record sources of information. The figures provided are an assembly of facts, estimates and some projections. Hopefully, they conservatively indicate actual current numbers.

In this "Story of Low German" I aspire to present the history of Low German and its relationship to the English language in a way that readers will find interesting and enjoyable.

Lay readers who like uncluttered pages will appreciate the absence of footnotes. Students seeking references, will find endnotes appended to the chapters. The notes explain and reinforce pertinent, controversial or misunderstood facts and events in this story. Most of the information has been derived from scholarly works referred to in the endnotes and in the bibliography. Such reference works provide greater detail and a broader perspective than can be provided in the condensed information on these few pages.

Many endnotes are written in German or refer to German publications simply because that is the language in which most reference literature about Low German is published. Consequently, those who read English only may enjoy the reading of this story, but may find it difficult to pursue the reference works quoted or to expand upon the information provided in it.

Acknowledgements

For their courtesy, assistance and advice I wish to thank the following people and organizations for their help to me in writing this "Story of Low German — and Plautdietsch":

— Kurt-Friedrich Bohrer of Mannheim, Germany for obtaining and sending copy of "Deutschsprachige Minderheiten, 1989."

— Ernst Christ of Norddeutscher Rundfunk, Kiel, Germany, for his written information on Low German radio programming by NDR, and listening audiences in northern Germany.

— Tjeerd de Graaf, Professor at the University of Groningen, for his letters and printed information on Low German, Frisian and Plautdietsch as spoken in Siberia.

— Barbara Grimes, Editor of Ethnologue, Hawaii, USA, for her information and advice on speakers of Low German world wide.

— Institut für Niederdeutsche Sprache, Bremen, Germany, whose personnel patiently and helpfully answered my numerous requests for information about Low German.

— Günter Kühn, Low German author, playwright and theatre director, Oldenburg, Germany, for his transcription into local dialect of a segment of literature in Chapter Eight.

— Jacob A. Loewen, Abbotsford, B.C., for supplying me with Walter Quiring's "Die Mundart von Chortitza in Süd-Rußland."

— Dieter Möhn, Professor at the University of Hamburg, Germany, for information about relevant publications and names and addresses of colleagues engaged in Low German studies.

— Hermann Niebaum, Professor at the University of Groningen, for information on the Lower Franconian (Flemish) dialects.

— Hans von Niessen, of Mennonitische Umsiedlerbetreuung, Neuwied, Germany, for his personal letter with information about numbers of speakers of Plautdietsch.

— STYX Publications of Groningen, Netherlands, for their kind permission to reprint portions of copyrighted literature from their 1991 publication "PLATTformen 91."

— Jack Thiessen, Professor of German (Emeritus), University of Winnipeg, for continually sending me information and publications about Low German and/or Plautdietsch.

— James Urry, author of "None but Saints" and Professor of Anthropology at Victoria University in Wellington, New Zealand, for his careful assistance with Mennonite history in Russia and the USSR.

— Norma Voth, author of "Mennonite Foods and Folkways from South Russia" for sending me Henry Dietrich Dyck's "Language Differentiation in two Low German Groups in Canada."

— Sebo Woldringh, Wycliffe Bible translators, Calgary, Alberta, for his assistance in providing statistics from "Ethnologue" on speakers of Low German.

— A special word of thanks is due to those here named who read draft copies of this "Story," made helpful suggestions and identified needed additions, deletions or revisions: Harry Loewen, Ernest and Amanda Epp, Darlene Funk, Peter and Anne Bargen, Karen and Cory Epp, Fred Froese, Jack Thiessen, Walter Klaassen, Joe Leask, and my wife Irmgard.

— to those persons, organizations and publications listed in the Endnotes and Bibliography, without whose information it would have been impossible to write this "Story of Low German—and Plautdietsch," I extend heart-felt thanks.

Reuben Epp

CHAPTER ONE

Introduction

The scholar who wrote, "English is a dialect of Low German,"[1] surely must have been joking. Or was he? The similarities between these languages and the common identities of their ancient peoples do not permit a sweeping rejection of this statement—despite its first-impression incredibility.

Tracing the English and Low German languages back to their roots of more than fifteen centuries ago, leads us to a people of Europe who spoke Old Saxon. A major contingent of them left the continent in the fifth century to settle on the island of Britain. The language of these settlers in Britain later became known as Old English; this same language, spoken by the people who remained on the mainland of Europe, became known as Old Low German.

Knowing that modern English and modern Low German both derive from these two "Old" languages with one common Old Saxon root, it becomes easier to understand why they today have so many words in common. "The Story of English"[2] tells us that the one hundred most commonly used words in English are of this "Old English" origin, also known as "Anglo-Saxon"; and that it is impossible to write a modern English sentence without using such words.

Similarities in the definitions of such terminologies as Old English, Anglo-Saxon, Old Saxon and Old Low German (the "Old" forms of modern English and Low German), permit us to understand that "Old Low German" has about the same meaning as "Anglo-Saxon" in the aforementioned statement from "The Story of English." Certainly, Old English words like *mann, hus* and *drincan* are almost identical to their equivalents in modern Low German. Many more words that are the same in English and Low German are listed in Chapter Four.

Some may wonder how it happened that Netherlandic Mennonites who immigrated to America from Russia speak a dialect of Low German. They may not know who Mennonites are. Or if they do, they may wonder just who or what is meant by netherlandic Mennonites.

This story traces the early growing period of Low German and of

1

English. It explores and explains the sibling affinity between these two languages. It explains who the Low German people are, who the netherlandic Mennonites are, where they came from and how they are linguistically and ethnically akin to the English.

Before we go into that, let us clear up some of the unfamiliar names and terms that we read about when looking into the story of Low German and the people who speak it. The following paragraphs explain such unfamiliar terminology, as well as other strange words and expressions to be encountered when reading about the history of the Low German language and its relationship to English.

Explanations and Definitions
of Terminology and Nomenclature

Low German

To many people, the term "Low German" does not have a clearly understood meaning. To some it means a "lower" or "less acceptable" form of German; to others it indicates a dialect of standard German that has been labelled "low German" to differentiate it from the recognized standard language of Germany.

Consequently, it may be surprising to learn that Low German is a language of its own,[3] that it held recognition and international status long before English or German. It played a prominent role in the affairs of northern Europe[4] before the English or German languages came into the general and widespread use for which they are known today.

Low German is one of the North Sea Germanic group of languages which, along with English and the Nordic languages, developed in lands bordering the shores of the North Sea.[5] It was and continues to be the language of the common people of northern Germany and parts of the Netherlands. In Germany it is spoken to the north of an irregular imaginary line running approximately from Düsseldorf through Göttingen from the west, and from there in a northeasterly direction toward Berlin and on to the border with Poland. In the Netherlands, where it is known as Nether Saxon, it is spoken in the northern Dutch provinces adjoining Germany. The official language of all of Germany is (High) German, but at one time centuries ago, the people of northern Germany spoke only Low German and knew no High German.

Encyclopædia Britannica describes one of the chief characteristics of Low German as the absence in it of the High German sound shift. In Low German and High German words that otherwise might be similar or identical, the "p" consonant in Low German frequently changes to "pf" or "ff" (Peper becomes Pfeffer) in High German. Similarly, the consonant "t" becomes "z", "tz", or "ss" (Water becomes Wasser). Some other consonants are also shifted, such as: "b>p", "d>t" and "g>k." This sound shift in consonants began in the High German South in about AD 500 and moved northward, but Low German remained untouched by it. In this respect, Low German agrees with Frisian and English.[6]

Encyclopædia Britannica charts two German languages and their divisions: Low German and High German, listing their various branches and components. Low German is shown to consist of two branches, namely: Low Franconian (Flemish, Dutch) and Low Saxon (Plattdeutsch).[7]

Low Franconian. This branch of Low German is also known in English as Lower Franconian or Nether Franconian and in German as Niederfränkisch. It is spoken as native dialect in the southern portion of the Netherlands (Holland) and in Belgium. Although there appears to be some sensitivity toward identifying it with the Low German language, some scholars nevertheless agree with this identity.[8] It is understandable that there be lack of agreement in identifying language and/or dialect at the western end of the Low German language zone in the Netherlands, because the lines of demarcation between Nether Saxon Low German and the Nether Franconian Flemish/Dutch are so gradual and diffused that scholars find it difficult (or impossible) to define where one language or dialect ends and the other begins.[9]

Low Saxon. The Low Saxon branch of the Low German language is also referred to as Lower Saxon or Nether Saxon. In German it is called Niedersächsisch or Plattdeutsch. The term Niederdeutsch is also used, but it has the broader connotation of encompassing the entire Low German language, including the Lower Saxon branch. Low Saxon is currently spoken in various dialects in the Netherlands and Germany from Groningen in the West to Mecklenburg and the former Pomerania in the East. Prior to the end of World War II, it was also spoken throughout West and East Prussia.

PLATTDEUTSCH AND/OR PLATT

Because the German word "platt" means the equivalent of the English word "flat," and "deutsch" means "German," a literal translation of "Plattdeutsch" would seem to be "flat German". Therefore, it is confusing to learn that "Plattdeutsch" is not intended to mean that at all.

The Low German author Fritz Specht in 1969 described the meaning of Plattdeutsch (here paraphrased in English), as follows:

Many believe that Plattdeutsch means the flat, lower or lesser language. Others—more friendly—believe that it is the language of the flat countryside of northern Germany. Neither of these definitions strike the mark. The designation "platt" goes back to a netherlandic word meaning: "clear, popular, understandable." One would use it to describe a transcription of the Bible into the vernacular. An invective, it certainly is not! In spite of that, some think that it is more genteel to use the expression "Niederdeutsch" (Nether-German) in place of "Plattdeutsch" (flat-German). But the meanings of both are essentially the same.[10]

To northern Germans or to speakers of Nether Saxon Low German, "Plattdeutsch" or "Platt" are commonly understood to mean "Nether Saxon." The word "Niederdeutsch" is also used, but usually only by

3

scholars and others in reference to the broader concept of Low German, as opposed to the Nether Saxon branch of it. For example: the term "Niederdeutsch" is used when referring to the Low German language or to Low German theatre or literature.[11]

The term "Platt" in this short form is occasionally heard to the south of the Low German region of Germany in describing local language that is not standard German.[12] In such case, it simply means "local dialect." But, in the extreme south of Germany a local dialect is called "Dialekt." Consequently, in discussing Low German with someone in or from southern Germany, correct understanding can be better ensured by using the term "Niederdeutsch" in place of "Plattdeutsch" or "Platt" when referring to "Low German."

HIGH GERMAN

What is generally understood to be High German is the standardized form of German found in literature, in business correspondence, in educational institutions and in official correspondence or communication. It has regional variations and differences because it is a "created" language that had no native home. Some Germans still regard it as a "curious newspaper language, unjustly termed to be High German."[13]

The standardized form of the High German language has grown from centuries of work by language scholars, authors, literary people and language departments of German universities. The translation of the Bible by Martin Luther into German became a major contribution toward standardizing a German language.[14]

The foremost authority on standard German and its use is considered to have been Konrad Duden, who died in 1911. His reference works are still published under the Duden name, intermittently reviewed by an Editorial Board who have the respect of users and scholars as "the authorities" on German.[15]

Although the usual designation for the High German standard language is simply German, the term "High" is frequently used herein to differentiate between Low German and standard German, which are two distinct and separate languages.

NETHERLANDIC MENNONITES

Since the term "Mennonite" describes a religion or members of a religious faith, without ethnical or language connotation, a Mennonite may be of any race, with any colour of skin and the speaker of any language. Therefore, there is no such thing as a Mennonite language or culture. On the other hand, there is a major contingent of people of the Mennonite faith, whose forefathers came from the netherlands some 450 years ago, who have some ethnicity and language in common.

Netherlandic Mennonites, including Flemish refugees, together with others from central and southern Germany and Switzerland, became the forebears of Mennonites now living in America, primarily on the prairies of western Canada and the United States, and in Mexico. A sizable contingent also lives on the Niagara peninsula of southern Ontario. (There are numerous non-netherlandic Mennonite congregations of High German and Swiss descent in Ontario and the eastern States). Over the centuries after AD 1550, several large contingents of these Mennonite forebears migrated from the netherlands to Polish Prussia, from there to New Russia (later to become the Ukraine), and subsequently to the Americas. Since the majority of these people who reached America via the Prussian and Russian route speak Low German, and are of a common netherlandic Frisian/Flemish background, they constitute an ethnic and religious group that can be described as netherlandic Mennonite.

On the other hand, some Mennonites did not leave the Netherlands in spite of oppression by the authorities of that time, and their descendants still live there. Among the Dutch they are known as Doopsgezinde (Baptism-minded ones—Anabaptists). Their congregations and churches are located in various places such as Amsterdam, Witmarsum, Leeuwarden, Groningen and Veendam. There are many more.

NETHERLANDS/NETHERLANDS

The term "Netherlands" has both geographical and political connotations. For purposes of describing Low German and movements of Mennonites, the meaning attached to the uncapitalized word "netherlands" as used henceforth in this chapter, is that which describes the countryside, its people and in some cases its language, regardless of political borders. For example: the geographic netherlands include the political Netherlands (also known as Holland), most of Belgium and the province (land) of East Friesland (Ostfriesland) of the northwest corner of Germany. East Friesland is part of the netherlandic area to which Unruh refers as the Frisia Triplex[16] (Map #1, p. 7).

When the term "netherlands" is used in this chapter in the geographical sense, it is not capitalized. Whenever the proper name "Netherlands" is used in connection with the political entity, also known as Holland, the name shall be properly capitalized. References to netherlandic Mennonites mean Mennonites whose forebears originally came from the Netherlands (Holland), from Flanders in Belgium or from East Friesland in Germany. A few also came from the Duchy (land or province) of Oldenburg which borders on East Friesland and has much in common with it.

It is substantially correct to refer to netherlandic Mennonites as Dutch Mennonites, even though they did not all originally come from the Netherlands (Holland). Those who came from Flanders and East Friesland were also Dutch because the Dutch language was used extensively throughout those areas at that time. In Flanders, Dutch is still in general use whereas in East Friesland the official language is now German.

FRISIAN/FRIESLAND

It is confusing to find two Frieslands on maps of northern Germany and the Netherlands. West Friesland lies in the northeastern corner of the Netherlands whereas East Friesland is part of northwestern Germany (Map #1, p. 7). Curiously, the two Frieslands are separated by the province of Groningen in the Netherlands, and by the international border between the Netherlands and Germany. It is no less confusing for the visitor to the two Frieslands to find that different languages are spoken in them.

Friesland. The Friesland that one finds on most maps of the Netherlands is actually West Friesland,[17] although mapmakers usually show it simply as Friesland. The Friesland shown on a map of Germany is usually shown as Ostfriesland (East Friesland), despite the fact that it is the most westerly province of northern Germany.

One might wonder why maps show a Friesland in the Netherlands (West Friesland), and an East Friesland in northwest Germany, with a Dutch province by the name of Groningen separating them. All political considerations aside, the provinces of West Friesland, Groningen and East Friesland have been occupied throughout recorded history by Frisian people. Consequently, these lands are correctly understood to constitute *Friesland*,[18] the historical and current homeland of Frisian people.[19]

This area is shown as Friesland by National Geographic[20] and is also referred to by historians and scholars as the Frisia Triplex ("Dreierfriesland" in German).[21] The two Frieslands together with Groningen form the Friesland called the "Frisia Triplex," which is the original homeland of the netherlandic Low German Mennonites. The term "Frisia Triplex" appears frequently in following chapters dealing with Frisian people and Mennonites.

Frisian. Frisian is the name of a people and their language. The name "Friesens" or "Frisians" in Gothic meant "Free Ones." The English Franciscan monk, Bartholomaeus Anglicus, wrote of them as a strong, rough people, proud of their freedom and peculiar customs. The Romans reported them as exceeding any other people in bravery and faithfulness.[22]

The Frisian people, who were heathen until the eighth century, had fiercely resisted attempts to christianize them by the Franks from the south. They first peacefully listened to the preaching of Wilfrid, bishop of York (Britain) in AD 678. Christianity was established in Frisia by the Englishman Willibrord, between AD 690 and 739. But, conversion of the heathen Frisians to Christianity, was not brought about quickly or en masse. This is borne out in the death of the English missionary Boniface as a martyr among them at Dokkum, Frisia in AD 754.[23]

The descendants of these Frisian people now make their homes in the Frisia Triplex, on the Frisian Islands and along the west coast of Schleswig-Holstein. In most of these areas, Frisian and Nether Saxon peoples have become almost indistinguishable.[24]

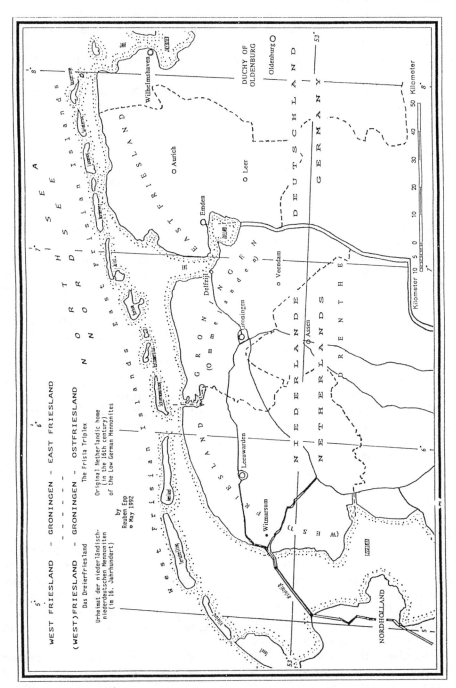

WEST FRIESLAND – GRONINGEN – EAST FRIESLAND
– – – – – –
(WEST)FRIESLAND – GRONINGEN – OSTFRIESLAND
The Frisia Triplex
Das Dreierfriesland

Urheimat der niederländisch-   Original Netherlandic home
niederdeutschen Mennoniten   (in the 16th century)
(im 16. Jahrhundert)   of the Low German Mennonites

by
Reuben Epp
© May 1992

Map #1

7

Frisian Language. The Frisian language, also referred to as Anglo-Frisian,[25] is the language of the Frisian people. In many respects it has a close resemblance to English.[26] In some of the traditional Frisian areas, such as West Friesland and some of the Frisian islands of the North Sea coasts, the Frisian people still proudly retain their Frisian language.[27]

In other areas, such as in the provinces of Groningen and East Friesland, Frisian and Nether Saxon peoples have assimilated each other, but the Low German of the Nether Saxons has become the dominant language among them.

NETHER SAXON/LOWER SAXONY

The term "Nether Saxon," synonymous with Low or Lower Saxon, describes a branch of the Low German language spoken not only in the current state of Lower Saxony in Germany, but in Schleswig-Holstein and in the eastern netherlandic provinces of Groningen, Drenthe and Overijssel. It is also spoken in Mecklenburg and northern East Germany, as it was until 1945 in the former Pomerania and Prussia.

Lower Saxony. Lower Saxony is a large administrative unit, known as Niedersachsen in German. It is a political division, somewhat equivalent to a province in Canada or a state in the United States. Its borders have changed as the results of wars and power struggles over the centuries. On modern maps of Germany, it is shown covering a large part of West Germany, much of which was formerly part of the Kingdom of Prussia, even in this century.

The administrative unit known as Lower Saxony now encompasses regions (lands or provinces) that at one time were independently ruled, such as East Friesland and Oldenburg, whose inhabitants speak a number of different dialects of the Lower Saxon branch of the Low German language.

When one reads of the dialect of Lower Saxony, what is meant is the dialect of an area near Hannover (Hanover) and Celle, traditionally known as Niedersachsen. It is only one of the dialects of Low German now spoken among the people who inhabit the greater administrative area known as Lower Saxony.

PRUSSIA

When discussing the Prussian language, the term "Prussia" means the original two provinces of the former Prussia, namely: West Prussia and East Prussia. This area included the Free City of Danzig and the territory administered by it until the collapse of Germany in 1945 (Maps #5, p. 66 & #6, p. 69). The "Prussia" referred to here is not that large portion of northern Germany known in the nineteenth century as the Kingdom of Prussia, which ended with the revolution of 1918.

Plautdietsch. At the time of the 16th century Mennonite resettlement from the Frisia Triplex to the delta of the Vistula River (then part of Poland which later became part of West Prussia), the resident peoples of

THE WESTERN GERMANIC GROUP OF LANGUAGES

This schematic simplistically represents the relationships between Frisian, English and Low German languages. Because the early story of these languages is obscured behind centuries of unrecorded or lost ancient history, any simple graphic design can only approximately depict those interwoven relationships. However, there is general agreement that today's English and Low German languages are directly descended from the Old Saxon of the Western Germanic family of Indo-European languages as here shown:

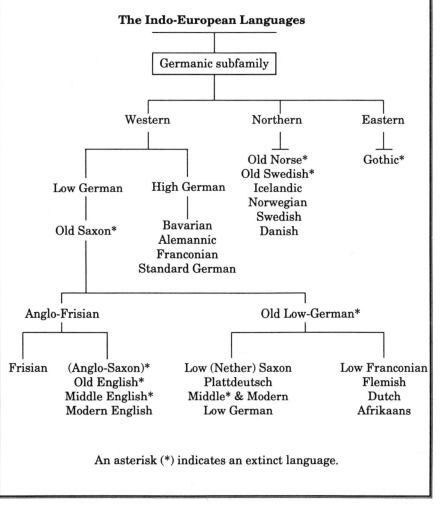

The Indo-European Languages

Germanic subfamily

Western — Northern — Eastern

Old Norse* — Gothic*

Low German — High German — Old Swedish*
Icelandic
Norwegian
Swedish
Old Saxon* — Bavarian — Danish
Alemannic
Franconian
Standard German

Anglo-Frisian — Old Low-German*

Frisian — (Anglo-Saxon)* — Low (Nether) Saxon — Low Franconian
Old English* — Plattdeutsch — Flemish
Middle English* — Middle* & Modern — Dutch
Modern English — Low German — Afrikaans

An asterisk (*) indicates an extinct language.

9

the delta among whom they settled, already spoke Nether Saxon (Nether Prussian) dialects similar to the netherlandic dialects spoken by the incoming Mennonites.[28] After the Mennonites were settled, they not only adapted their own manner of speech to that of their new neighbours, but also imparted to it more than one hundred netherlandic words. This varied dialectical amalgam became the Plautdietsch of the netherlandic Mennonites in Prussia which they carried with them in subsequent movements to various other parts of the world.

This Low German dialect of the Vistula area was spoken, not only by the minority Mennonites,[29] but also by the resident population. Consequently, there are former non-Mennonite residents of West Prussia who, together with their descendants, also speak Plautdietsch and similar dialects. Therefore, the term "Mennonite Plautdietsch" is herein used to describe the Low German language of those netherlandic Mennonites whose forefathers participated in the Prussian/Russian sojourn, but without treating it as exclusively their dialect.

Nether Prussian. The term "Niederpreußisch" (Nether Prussian) descriptively classifies the Low German dialects of East and West Prussia without minimizing their Nether Saxon Low German orientation. Ziesemer lists nine different dialects of Low German in Prussia, among which the Plautdietsch of the Mennonites fits in with what he describes as that of the Nehrung and Werder.[30] The Nether Prussian dialects have some "Prussian" peculiarities about them that set them apart from their sister dialects of the eastern Low German language family outside of Prussia.

Scholars classify the Prussian Low German dialects as "Niederpreußisch, Niedersächsisch-niederpreußisch" (Nether Prussian, Nether-Saxon-Nether-Prussian).[31] Thiessen describes the Nether Prussian dialect of the Mennonites (Plautdietsch) as a Lower Saxon vernacular.[32]

NOTES TO CHAPTER ONE

Note: The descriptions of texts repeatedly referred to in these notes, after being once identified, shall thereafter be abbreviated, as follows:

Reference Text	Abbrev.
B.H. Unruh, *Die niederländisch-niederdeutschen Hintergründe zur Mennonitischen Ostwanderungen,* (Karlsruhe: Im Selbstverlag, 1955)	*Unruh*
Gerhard Cordes und Dieter Möhn, *Handbuch zur niederdeutschen Sprach- und Literaturwissenschaft,* (Berlin: Erich Schmidt Verlag, 1983)	*NSL*
Horst Penner, *Die ost- und westpreußischen Mennoniten,* (Weierhof: Mennonitischer Geschichtsverein, 1978)	*Penner*
Dieter Stellmacher, *Niederdeutsche Sprache,* (Langs Germanistische Lehrbuchsammlung, Band 26, (Bern: Verlag Peter Lang AG, 1990)	*NS*

1. Christopher Moss, *Niederdeutsch-englische Sprachzusammenhänge,* "Handbuch zur niederdeutschen Sprach- und Literaturwissenschaft," (Berlin: Erich Schmidt Verlag, 1983),

p. 660. Moss writes as follows: "Die gemeinsamen Ursprünge der engl. und der nd. Sprache werfen automatisch das Problem der Historizität auf. Bense schreibt: "As English is itself a Low German Dialect, we prefer to use the term *Low Dutch* in reference to the sister dialects . . . which are usually distinguished by the names *Flemish, Dutch and Low German.*" Ref: (Bense, J.F.: A Dictionary of the Low Dutch Element in the English Vocabularly. The Hague, 1939).

2. Robert McCrum, William Cran and Robert MacNeil, "The Story of English," (New York: Viking Penguin Incorporated, 1986), p. 61.

3. Karl Fissen, *Plattdütsch Läwt!*, (Oldenburg: Heinz Holzberg Verlag, 1963), p. 54.
   —Fritz Specht, *Plattdeutsch wie es nicht im Wörterbuch steht*, (Frankfurt: Verlag Heinrich Scheffler, 1969), p. 11.

4. Fissen, p. 10.
   —Artur Gabrielsson, *"Die Verdrängung der mnd. Sprache,"* *NSL*, pp. 119-120.

5. Christopher Moss, "Niederdeutsch-englische Sprachzusammenhänge," *NSL*, p. 661.

6. *Encyclopædia Britannica*, "German Language," (Chicago, William Benton, 1959), Vol. 10, p. 214c.

7. *Ibid.*, Vol. 10, p. 215a.

8. Heinz Kloss: In a personal letter to the writer regarding his assertion that Low German is spoken in Flanders, Kloss responds on the 26th July 1986: "Auf einen kleinen Irrtum darf ich Sie aufmerksam machen: In Flandern (Flanders) wird kein Low German gesprochen; Vlaams ist die Bezeichnung für . . . die in Belgien gesprochene regionalen Dialekte . . . die aber weder in Belgien noch in Westdeutschland als Dialekte der niederdeutschen Sprache gelten".
   —Compare this then with the following:
   —*Encycl. Brit.*, "German Language," Vol. 10, p. 215a.
   —Dieter Stellmacher, "Phonologie und Morphologie," *NSL*, p. 240. "Als ein dritter Dialektraum des Niederdeutschen wird oft noch das Niederfränkische gewertet . . . "
   —Unruh, p. 16. "eigentlich gehört zu dem 'Niederdeutschen' auch das 'Niederfränkische'." p. 180. "Wissenschaftlich teilt man das Niederdeutsche in das Niederfränkische (Flämisch-Holländische) und in das Niedersächsische."

9. Dieter Stellmacher, "Neuniederdeutsche Grammatik," *NSL*, p. 239.

10. Specht, p. 11
    —Fissen, p. 46.

11. Stellmacher, *NS*, p. 14.

12. Stellmacher, *NS*, p. 14.

13. Egon Monk, *Niederdeutsch Heute*, Institut fur niederdeutsche Sprache, (Leer: Schuster Verlag Leer, 1976), p. 179.

14. *Encycl. Brit.*, "German Language," 1959, Vol. 10, pp. 214-216.

15. *Der Große Duden*, (Mannheim: Bibliographisches Institut, 1961).

16. Unruh, pp. 7-10.

17. *Ibid.*, p. 15.

18. The only map in the possession of this writer, showing Friesland as the combined area which, on most other maps appears as Friesland, Groningen and East Friesland, is the Map Supplement to the National Geographic, September 1991, Page 2A, Vol.180 No. 3
    —Germany, (Washington, D.C: National Geographic Magazine, 1991).

19. Unruh, pp. 6-10. Unruh states that the Frisians, having apparently come to Friesland from farther north, at one time occupied lands far beyond the current Friesland. He further states that it is not well enough known that about half of the land of Schleswig was at one time populated by Frisians.

20. See note #18 above.

21. *Ibid.*, p. 7.

11

22. *Ibid.*, p. 8.

23. *Encycl. Brit.,* "England, Church of," 1959, Vol. 8, p. 467a.
    —*Ibid.*, "Frisians," 1959, Vol. 9, p. 854a.

24. Unruh, pp. 13-15.

25. Unruh, p. 13.

26. *Encycl. Brit.,* "Frisians," 1959, Vol. 9, p.854b

27. Bogdan Zaborski, "European Languages, (Map)," *World Book Atlas,* (Chicago: World Book Encyclopedia, Inc., Rand McNally & Co., 1981), p. 144.

28. Penner, p. 180.

29. W.W. Moelleken, *Die linguistische Heimat der Rußlandeutschen Mennoniten in Kanada und Mexico,* Niederdeutsches Jahrbuch, Jahrgang 1987, (Neumünster: Karl Wachholtz Verlag, 1987, p. 94.

30. Walther Ziesemer, *Die Ostpreussischen Mundarten,* (Wiesbaden: Dr. Martin Sändig oHG., 1970), p. 137.

31. Dieter Stellmacher, *Niederdeutsch - Formen und Forschungen,* (Tübingen: Max Niemeyer Verlag, 1981), p. 112.
    —Penner, p. 180.
    —Stellmacher, *NS*, p. 137.

32. Jack Thiessen, "The Low German of the Canadian Mennonites," *Mennonite Life*, July 1967, p. 110.

CHAPTER TWO

The History of Low German—Part I

An understanding of the relationship between Low German and other languages depends on knowing about its colourful and varied past. The roots of Low German go back as far as, or farther than those of German, and considerably farther than those of English which also has major roots in the Old Saxon language, the ancient progenitor of Low German.

The foregoing simply-stated perspective on the relationship between English and Low German provides only a glimpse of the story that emerges when looking into the history of the two.

The roots of the Saxon language go back to the North Sea Germanic[1] (also called Ingvaeonic) languages, a branch of the Germanic language group. This branch developed in lands near the North Sea and was the primogenitor from which today's Low German, Dutch, Nordic and English languages emerged in various stages.[2]

Some may disagree with the simplistic assertion that English is descended from Low German.[3]

But, it cannot be denied that pursuing the "Old" source of either language reveals the roots of the other. Therefore, a review of the history of Old Low German also reviews the history of Old English for the same period.

Anglo-Saxon Roots of English

Many readers are familiar with the occupation of Britain by the Angles and the Saxons about fifteen centuries ago. Some probably also know that the Anglo-Saxon occupation of Britain was joined by the Frisians and the Jutes. The following paragraphs will attempt to identify those various peoples and explain where they came from.

THE ANGLES

Not much is known of the Angles (also known as Angli) as a people before they became known in the occupation of Britain. According to the historian Bede and "Historia Brittonum," the Angles in Britain came from an area at that time known as Angulus. King Alfred and the chronicler Aethelweard identified their place of origin as Angel (Angeln), in what we now know as the province of Schleswig of northern Germany [4]

THE SAXONS

The Saxon people derived their "Saxon or Sassen" name from their short sword, called the "sahs," by which they were then recognized.[5] They are first known, in the second century,[6] to have lived north of the Elb river of Germany, in the area now known as Holstein.[7] In the fourth century and thereafter, they spread southward and westward, overrunning areas populated by other peoples who more or less accepted their intrusions with acquiescence. By the second half of the fourth century, Saxons had settled in West Flanders and in Normandy, groups of them having ventured and settled as far west as the mouth of the Loire river of western France, whence the area derived the name "litus Saxonicum."[8]

THE FRISIANS

The Frisian people were found by the Romans in the first century occupying the coastal lands of what we today describe as the Netherlands.[9] In fact, they also occupied other coastlands, especially the North Sea coastal islands farther east and north toward Denmark. They were a people whose language and culture differed somewhat from those of the Saxons, and they had a reputation for being proud and independent. At the time of the occupation of Britain, large areas of their traditional homelands had been overrun by Saxons moving westward. Frisian people (with some Saxon infusion) still occupy the province of West Friesland in the Netherlands and some North Sea coastal islands. They proudly speak their own Frisian language.

THE JUTES

The Jutes were another of the Germanic (Teutonic) tribes from continental Europe who participated in the occupation of Britain. Bede, who calls them Iutae or Iuti,[10] says that the land of the Angles lay between that of the Saxons and the Iutae. This would place the original homeland of the Jutes on the peninsula of Jutland, the continental portion of Denmark.

THE OCCUPATION OF BRITAIN

The western outposts of the Saxons along the coast of Normandy in all likelihood served as ports of embarkation for the sea journey across the English Channel in the fifth century movement to Britain.[11] This migration by the Saxons was joined by Angles and Jutes from farther north on the peninsula of Jutland (Denmark). There is evidence to indicate that Frisians also joined the movement to Britain. This probability is supported by the close resemblance between the Frisian and English languages.[12]

Although some scholars and historians refer to the Anglo-Saxon occupation of Britain as an invasion, there is considerable historical evidence to show that the resident Celts in Britain invited tribes from the continent to help them fight off attacks by the Picts and the Scots from the north.[13] Some historians also assert that once there, the Saxons and others indeed fought off the attackers from the north, but then turned on the Celts and forced them to the west (Wales). The purpose of this writing is not to prove or disprove invasion theories, but to relate what took place in regard to the migration of people from the continent to the island of Britain, and what took place after that in the language of peoples in both places. Consequently, the term "occupation" is here used to tell about the Anglo-Saxon migration to Britain. Those who prefer to interpret it as an "invasion," are hereby not constrained.

The occupation of Britain by Angles, Saxons and Jutes began about AD 449[14] and, as mentioned, was joined by Frisians among the occupiers.[15] Nothing has been found to indicate that there was any difference in race between the Angles and the Saxons. The Jutes may have been of a somewhat different race, but it is doubtful that their Germanic language diverged to any extent from that of the others.[16]

Anglo-Saxon England

The term Anglo-Saxon in English history applies to that period of time after the occupation of Britain by the Angles and the Saxons, but preceding the Norman conquest. There is lack of distinction between Angles and Saxons of those times because West Saxon writers spoke of themselves as Angelcyn and their language as Englisc,[17] while the West Saxon royal family claimed to be of the stock of Bernicia. We need not doubt that the Angles and Saxons had practically coalesced, perhaps even before the occupation.[18]

No fundamental differences at that time separated Angles, Saxons and Jutes, even though they may have been of distinct origin. Their cultures appear to have been the same, and any language differences can only have been slight in the seventh century. There was a general uniformity in English culture of the earliest period.[19]

The occupation of Britain by the Angles, Saxons, Jutes and Frisians in the fifth century was of such magnitude, and their activities there so extensive, that the island of Britain became the major centre for further development of the Old Saxon language and the culture of the people who spoke it.

During the early centuries of Angles and Saxons in Britain they spoke a language that we refer to in today's terminology as Old English or Anglo-Saxon, which terms seem relatively synonymous. Old English continued to evolve, as languages do, until the Norman conquest of 1066 initiated an era that brought major French influences into the language of Britain. The period that followed is today referred to as Middle English. It lasted until about AD 1500 when the introduction of printing ushered in a new era of language development now called the period of Modern English.

The history of the English language divides chronologically into three main periods, represented as follows:

1. The Old English (Anglo-Saxon) Period (AD 450 - 1050)
2. The Middle English Period (AD 1050 - 1500)
3. The Modern English Period (AD 1500 —)

Roots of the Low German Language

While the English language in Britain progressed through the foregoing periods of development in its history, the Low German language was developing in similar but different stages in its time. Modern scholars similarly allocate to its history three periods somewhat equivalent to those in the evolution of English.

DEVELOPMENTAL PERIODS IN LOW GERMAN

1. The Old Period (AD 450 - 1200)
   a. The Old Saxon Period (AD 450 - 800)
   b. The Old Low German Period (AD 800 - 1200)
2. The Middle Low German Period (AD 1200 - 1650)
3. The Modern Low German Period (AD 1850 —)

Such tabulation oversimplifies the involved and interesting story of Low German. Although scholars agree that the history of the Low German language has an "Old" period, it is observed that within the Old Period a transition from Old Saxon to Old Low German took place, dividing it into the two segments shown as a. and b.

Old Saxon/Old Low German Period

Scholars now generally agree that the first portion of the Old period for Low German should be termed Old Saxon,[21] a period during which the Old Saxon language may be regarded as "emerging Low German,"[22] but, nevertheless, still quite Old Saxon.[23]

Old Saxon. The Old Saxon portion of Low German history is considered to have begun in the fifth century. That was the time when many Saxons left the continent to occupy lands on the British Isles. The period continues throughout a time when those Saxons remaining on the continent had not yet come under the influence of the Franks and the Carolingian dynasty in the eighth century.

Old Low German. The second portion of the Old period is defined by Stellmacher as beginning about AD 800 and ending about AD 1200.[24] This epoch is recognized as the one which generated the most examples of Old Low German literature still in existence. In this connection it is regretfully known that entire libraries and archives of Old Low German literature, formerly stored at cultural and religious centres in Germany, have not been preserved. The best example of such literature to survive to our time is a religious (Christian) poem entitled "Heliand," consisting of some six thousand verses. It is a literary and period treasure, written by an unknown author about AD 850. A second example, also by an unknown author of about the same time, is "Genesis" which survives only in fragments.[25]

Shift of Centre of Activities. During the Old Saxon Period, the centre of gravity for Saxon peoples underwent a major shift. The movement of Saxon and Angle people from the continent to Britain, and their subsequent activities there, were of such magnitude that the move constituted a relocation of the cultural and language centre of the Saxon (Ingvaeonic) people. Those who remained on the continent thereafter were left in the minority, and were then on the peripheral fringes of the new nucleus and centre of activities in Britain.[26]

Christianization of the Saxons. During the Old Low German Period, at about the turn of the eighth into the ninth centuries, the continental Saxons and Frisians were christianized by British missionaries who had not forgotten their kinship with their racial brethren on the continent. Conversions to Christianity usually began with the nobility. In such cases, a noble would be required to recant his former heathen belief by oath, and then to personally testify in his own mother tongue of his new christian faith. Curiously, copies of the Old Saxon baptismal vow are a mixture of English and Low German, intended for Saxons, but having been written by a foreign (British) missionary, barely striking the Saxon mark.[27]

Summary of Chapter Two

The English and Low German languages both stem from the Old Saxon language whose roots lie in the North Sea Germanic of the Western Germanic language group.

In the fifth century, a large segment of Angles and Saxons from the continent of Europe, who spoke the Old Saxon language, took over occupation of those parts of the island of Britain that later came to be known as England. During the following centuries, the Old Saxon language in Britain evolved in stages that we now know as Old English (or Anglo-Saxon), Middle English and Modern English. The Old Saxon language spoken among those Saxons who remained on the continent, evolved through similar stages which we now call Old Saxon, Old Low German, Middle Low German and Modern Low German.

The magnitude of the Anglo-Saxon occupation of Britain (England) and the extent of their activities there, were sufficiently great to shift the main cultural and language centre among Saxon peoples from their former areas on the European continent to the new settlements in Britain.

Christianization and its accompanying advances in education and culture were first brought to the Saxons on the continent through British missionaries whose memories of their racial kinfolk on the continent they had not lost in the intervening centuries.

17

NOTES TO CHAPTER TWO

Note: Refer to endnotes of Chapter One for Abbreviations

1. Robert Claiborne, *Our Marvelous Native Tongue*, (Toronto: Random House of Canada, 1983), p. 72.

2. Ingerid Dal, "Altniederdeutsch und seine Vorstufen," *NSL*, p. 90.
   —*Encyclopædia Britannica*, "English Language," (Chicago: William Benton, Publisher, 1959), Vol. 8, p. 555d.

3. *Encycl. Brit.*, "English Language," 1959, Vol. 8, p. 555d.

4. *Encycl. Brit.*, "Angli," 1959, Vol.1, p. 931a.
   —Mc Crum, Cran and MacNeil, *The Story of English*, (New York: Viking Penguin Inc., 1986), p. 57.
   —Claiborne, *Our Marvelous Native Tongue*, p. 76.

5. Hermann Böning, *Plattdeutsches Wörterbuch*, (Verlag Heimatverein Herrlichkeit Dinklage e.V., 2. Auflage, 1970), p. 90. *Sasse, Sachse; sassisch, sächsisch.

6. Stellmacher, *NS*, p. 20.

7. Ingerid Dal, "Altniederdeutsch und seine Vorstufen," *NSL*, p. 79.

8. *Ibid.*, p. 79.

9. *Encycl. Brit.*, "Frisian," 1959, Vol. 9, pp. 854-855.

10. *Encycl. Brit.*, "Jutes," 1959, Vol. 13., p. 217.

11. Ingerid Dal, "Altniederdeutsch und seine Vorstufen," *NSL.*, p. 79.

12. *Encycl. Brit.*, "Frisians," 1959, Vol. 9, p. 854.
    —Unruh, p. 13.

13. *Encycl. Brit.*, "Britain," 1959, Vol. 4, p. 165b.
    —Claiborne, *Our Marvelous Native Tongue*, p. 74.

14. Robert McCrum, et al, *The Story of English*, p. 60.

15. *Encycl. Brit.*, "Frisians," 1959, Vol. 9, p. 854.
    —Unruh, p. 5.

16. *Encycl. Brit.*, "English Language," 1959, Vol. 8, p. 556.
    —*Encycl. Brit.*, "Anglo-Saxons," 1959, Vol. 1, p. 949.
    —Claiborne, *Our Marvelous Native Tongue*, p. 76.

17. McCrum, et al, *The Story of English*, p. 61.
    —Robert Claiborne, *Our Marvelous Native Tongue*, p. 70.

18. *Encycl. Brit.*, "Anglo-Saxons," 1959, Vol. 1, p. 949c

19. *Encycl. Brit.*, "English History," 1959, Vol. 8, p. 481a

20. *Encycl. Brit.*, "English Language," 1959, Vol. 8, pp. 556-561.
    —*World Book Encyclopedia*, "English Language," 1978, Vol. 6, pp. 248-249.

21. Stellmacher, *NS*, p. 19.

22. Ingerid Dal, "Altniederdeutsch und seine Vorstufen," *NSL*, p. 79.

23. *Ibid*, p. 78. According to Dal: Bede (Beda, Baeda), A.D. 672-735 and Alcuin, A.D. 735-804, referred in their writings to the Saxons remaining on the continent after many of them had resettled into Britain, as 'antiqui (vetuli) Saxones'.

24. Stellmacher, *NS*, p. 19.

25. Wolfgang Huber, "Altniederdeutsche Dichtung," *NSL*, p. 338.
    —Stellmacher, *NS*, p. 21.

26. Ingerid Dal, "Altniederdeutsch und seine Vorstufen," *NSL*, p. 87.

27. Stellmacher, *NS*, pp. 21-21.

CHAPTER THREE

The History of Low German—Part II

The Middle Low German Period[1]

The Middle Low German (Mittelniederdeutsch) period is the name that most appropriately defines the period of history of the Low German language which lies between Old Low German and Modern Low German. In former times, the designation of this period saw names such as düdesch, (nedder-)sassesch, nedderlendesch and oostersch competing with each other. The Middle Low German period divides into three subdivisions,[2] namely:

1. The Early Period (AD 1200 - 1350)
2. The Classical Period (AD 1350 - 1550)
3. The Late Period (AD 1550 - 1650)

The twelfth century, which is included in the latter part of the Old Saxon/Old Low German Period, represents a period of transition from Old Low German to Early Middle Low German. No representative literature survives from that period. The story of the Middle Low German period tends to give the Hanseatic League full credit for advancing the prominence of Low German through widespread use of it in its business and diplomatic activities. But, it must not be overlooked that Low German was much used in important circles outside of the League at that time. Furthermore, the successful operations of the League began in the Latin language, which was later replaced by Low German.[3]

THE HANSEATIC LEAGUE

Although it is impossible to pinpoint a year in which the Hanseatic League began, the cities of Hamburg and Lübeck entered an agreement in 1241 to protect the sea road connecting the North Sea and the Baltic. Then in 1256, the first known meeting of the "maritime towns" Hamburg, Lübeck, Lüneburg, Wismar, Rostock and Stralsund took place.[4] They later became known as the Wendish group. Since they participated in the first meeting to presage formation of the Hanseatic League and were among its leading cities, they may be regarded as the League's charter members.

The Hanseatic League was a business association of north German cities with port access to the North Sea and the Baltic Sea. Although agreements reached among these cities served the intent of economic improvement and advantage for the League's member cities, it was also normal business practice for members of the League to resort to political and diplomatic pressure, even warfare, to achieve its ends. The League made agreements to acquire exclusive rights to trade areas, to boycott and restrain trade of non-members, to obtain preferential treatment in the levying of taxes or duties on its members, and to prevent outside traders from trading in areas or goods the League had reserved as the mandate of its members.

The Golden Age of the Hansa. From the twelfth to the fourteenth centuries, the Teutonic Order of Knights had a great impact upon the fortunes of the Hanseatic League by placing German colonists in expanses of sparsely-populated Slavic territories eastward and northward along the Baltic coasts.[5] This expansion by Germans toward the East (Drang nach Osten) reached along the shores of the Baltic Sea as far east and north as today's city of St. Petersburg. Port cities and trading centres built by Germans along Baltic coasts became participants in the commerce of the Hanseatic League. Consequently, east-west dimensions of the League's trading area spanned across northern Europe from Brügge in Flanders to Novgorod in Russia. With the addition of a business counter in London, England (the Steelyard), and another in Bergen, Norway, the League came to exert its presence in all countries bordering the North Sea and the Baltic, including Scandinavian and other European Nordic countries (Map #2, p. 21). During the heyday of its existence, membership in the Hanseatic League totalled about seventy to seventy-seven cities.[6] (An official League count was never released).

The Golden Age of Low German. It is a fact of history that the activities of the Hanseatic League had a profound and far-reaching effect on use of the Low German language. During the League's period of affluence and power, Low German was the most important and widely-used international language of northern Europe.[7] Lübeck, the League's central office, was a Low German city doing business in various countries at that time.

Other leading cities and alternate meeting centres for the League's member cities such as Hamburg and Visby, were similarly Low German. Offices (counters) of the League in places such as London, Bergen and Novgorod were staffed by Low German personnel drawn from member cities. Counters of the League consisted of Low German business communities within cities in foreign countries, usually walled off from the local population. Consequently, the business language of the League in its offices was Low German, regardless of the language of the host country.[8]

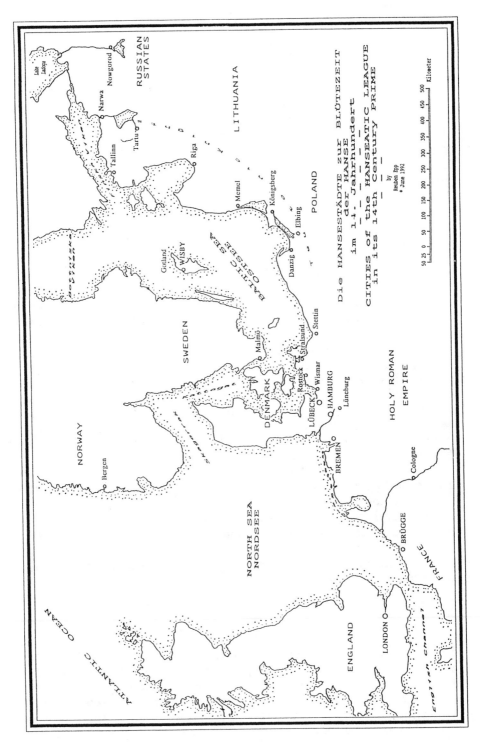

Map #2

Since Lübeck was the business and administrative centre of the Hanseatic League, the Low German used by the League was that of Lübeck.[9] This had the effect of standardizing spoken and written Low German in the business circles of member cities. This Low German of Lübeck orientation, became the language of law and authority, of administration, of business, of recorded history and of religious devotion.[10] By the middle of the fourteenth century it had displaced Latin and other languages for these functions in the German speaking and Nordic cities of Europe.[11] Low German had progressed to become northern Europe's language of big business, in use from Brügge to Riga and from Bergen to Novgorod.[12]

In the year AD 1366, the kings of Sweden and Denmark signed a treaty written in Low German. It determined the future of the Island of Gotland and was dated as follows: "drutteynhundert vnde in deme sesvndesestighesten iare"[13] (thirteen hundred and in the six and sixtieth year). On a famous code of Maritime Law, bearing the name of Visby on the Island of Gotland, the Low German title reads as follows: "Waterrecht dat de Kooplüde en de Schippers gemakt hebben to Visby"[14] (Water rights that the merchants and the shippers have made at Visby). The Peace of Stralsund in 1370, an agreement concluded between the Hanseatic League, the Privy Council of Denmark, Sweden, the Holsteiners and the Jutland nobles, was negotiated and concluded in the Low German language. This treaty granted great commercial privileges to the Hanseatic cities, and brought the League to the zenith of its power.[15] When the League later felt threatened by the powers of certain princes, against whom they could expect no help from a weakling central German government, they formed an opposing alliance in AD 1418, known as the "Tohopesate" (together-putting).[16]

In the century between AD 1325 and AD 1425, the Low German language had gained such prominence in the business communities of Denmark and southern Sweden, that these two countries considered authorizing Low German as their written business language, and in fact, nearly did so. But, this did not come to pass because the ordinary folk in each country would not give up their native dialects. Instead, the indigenous language became more standardized and was used increasingly more in writing and among the educated until it gradually gained acceptance.[17]

THE ECLIPSE OF THE
HANSEATIC LEAGUE

The merchants of the Hanseatic League had built a mighty business empire, reaching from Flanders to Russia and from London to Bergen and to Riga (Map #2, p. 21). But, in the sixteenth century, the traders of the League, known in the fourteenth century for their venturesome dealings, confronted a changing business world with methods proven in former centuries, but which were no longer appropriate. Such outmoded strategies proved to be impossible.[18]

The power politics of Christian II, king of Denmark, Norway and Sweden, threatened the interests of the Hanseatic League. His ruthless military campaigns placed him in opposition to the League and to the nobility of Sweden. A revolt led by Gustave Eriksson Vasa of Sweden brought about his defeat in 1521. Thereafter, the wise negotiations of the Bürgermeister of Lübeck, Thomas von Wickede, once more led the way to an agreement in 1523 between the new rulers Gustave Vasa of Sweden and Friedrich I of Denmark-Norway to reconfirm Hanseatic privileges in Scandinavia.

Although both kings owed their crowns to Lübeck, they soon thereafter followed their own nationalistic interests and permitted the passage of Dutch traders into the Baltic, the traditionally exclusive domain of the Hansa. The result was that, within the few decades leading to 1565, the Dutch became masters of 86% of Baltic Sea trade and 92% of that with Emden.[19] Last ditch attempts by the city of Lübeck to regain dominance for itself and for the Hansa by military action against Denmark in 1534-1536 failed miserably. Lübeck's military failure placed Denmark in a position of power supremacy in the Baltic for the next hundred years. For the Hanseatic League, this was devastating.[20]

In other countries the Hanseatic league came under increasing pressures from the growing powers of ruling princes. In 1494 the Hansa had already impotently witnessed the closing of the Hanseatic counter at Novgorod by Czar Ivan III. When in 1553 the English discovered a northern trade route to the northern Dwina estuary in Russia, over which they developed a lively sea trade,[21] King Edward VI declared all Hanseatic privileges in England annulled. An attempt by the Roman emperor in 1597 to restrict trade of the English "Merchant Adventurers" resulted in the 1598 closing by Queen Elisabeth of the Steelyard. This well-known counter of the Hanseatic League in London had been operating there continuously for over three hundred years.[22]

Such economic vacancies left by business disasters of the League, were seized upon as opportunities by a strong and vigorous commercial opposition operating from southern German cities. Foreign traders of the city of Nürnberg soon opened offices in Cologne, Lübeck and Danzig. Importers in Augsburg brought in copper from Hungary and gave the League lively competition to their trade in Swedish copper. Leipzig became the leader, ahead of Lübeck, in the fur trade with Russia. The Dutch fishing trade and English textile industries opened western trading doors into regions of Germany and northern Europe that had been until then controlled and dominated by the League.[23]

In the South of Germany lay also the greatest threat to the language and culture of the North—the High German language, customs and culture.[24] Just how serious this threat was to the language and culture of northern Germany and northern Europe was to make itself known in due time, in most respects—permanently!

THE DECLINE OF LOW GERMAN

The collapse of the business empire of the Hanseatic league adversely affected the lives of many people all over northern Germany and elsewhere. What had been a tower of economic strength for Low German business people, the patron of their livelihoods, their language and their culture, became frail and finally ended ignominiously. This eventually caused a loss of confidence among northerners in their own society, their culture and their language. When failure induces a society to lose confidence in itself, it becomes vulnerable to accepting the culture and language of a more successful society.[25]

In this case, the more successful society was the High German South which had outcompeted their Hansa. Among people of northern Germany, the more affluent after about AD 1500 were those from the South who brought with them High German customs and spoke the High German language. For a northerner (speaker of Low German) to get a good job and to be well accepted in society in the new order of things, it became important to be acquainted with High German manners and customs and to speak the language fluently. Consequently, in the sixteenth century it became customary for business people of Hamburg to send their sons to Leipzig for their training "for the sake of the language."[26]

It was also a time when many northern families high-germanized "verhochdeutscht" their family names. For example: a family with the Low German name Wienbarg might change it to Weinberg, which had the same meaning, but in those times sounded "more sophisticated." Similarly, the name Pötker might be changed to Töpfer. So naive were some of the people in changing their names that they occasionally settled for half a change and ended up with a name half Low German and half High German, such as Grothausen, Schumaker or Wittenberg.[27]

The loss of confidence in things Low German and the desire to strive for what seemed more desirable was not confined to the business world, but carried over into most spheres of interest and social activities. Although the Low German language continued to be spoken by common people throughout the north, the change to High German outside of the home or the workplace was gradually but inescapably coming into vogue.

The Transition Period

The attitudes which brought about the decline of the Low German language also engendered a period of transition from the use of Low German to the use of High German, in business and social circles, and particularly in writing. It also introduced a period of dialectalization of the Low German language which was most concentrated in the sixteenth century, but which must have lasted much longer.

During this period of transition there were no particular proclamations or formulated policies of governing bodies that brought about change from one language to another.[28] The change took place quite spontaneously, but slowly. It was brought about by reasons which stemmed from the collapse of the Hanseatic League.[29] Neither the former prosperity of the Hansa nor its well-developed language of business were any longer in demand. The time for change had come, the people yielded to it, and the changeover from Low German to High German proceeded slowly, progressively and inexorably, over several centuries.

Literature. Although the Golden Age of Low German saw the language used in all forms of literature, and abundantly so, once public attitude had become conditioned to the decline of Low German and the ascent of High German, Low German literature ceased to be written. The last Low German play of literary rank during that period was a religious drama entitled "De düdesche Schlömer" (The Low German Reveller) written by Johannes Stricker in 1584. After that, no Low German literature of comparable literary quality appeared for more than two and one half centuries.[30] Printing in Low German reached its lowest ebb of the seventeenth century in the year 1680. What was then printed was mainly humour, slap-stick comedy and limericks intended for entertainment at functions such as weddings.[31]

Princely Courts. As happened in the change from Latin to Low German as the language of diplomacy in the Hanseatic World, the princely courts again led the way in the changeover to the new High German idiom. Whereas the Treaty of Gotland in 1366, and the Treaty of Stralsund in 1370 were written in Low German, the Treaty of Bromsebro in 1541 and the Treaty of Stettin in 1570 were written in High German.[32]

City Governments. The conversion from Low German to High German in city administrations, local justice systems and record keeping by various departments of city governments, depended in their timing on a number of factors. Those departments handling external communications usually received first priority in the changeover, whereas departments handling only internal communications changed last. Geographic location of a city also affected the urgency and rapidity of change. The language of the court in Lüneburg, for example, had completely converted to High German by 1600, whereas in Hamburg similar change was not completed until 20 years later. In Emden a number of Guild books were kept in Low German until the year 1700.[33]

Church and School. In the schools and churches, the change in language of instruction or preaching was confronted with the problem of ensuring that people, whose lives were steeped in Low German, understood the new idiom. Although this was not necessarily always achieved, it is recorded that the changeover to High German in schools and churches in the larger cities was substantially completed by the middle of the seventeenth century.[34]

PUBLIC ATTITUDES TO THE
LANGUAGE QUESTION

The attitude of some segments of the German-speaking population toward use of Low German or High German is so intertwined with historic events that it is difficult to determine whether one caused the other, or whether change and attitude developed together. In either case, the record of those times not only documents the language change from Low German to High German, but also some of the attitudes accompanying that change. Tragic commentary on perceptions of some "educated" minds, even in this century, are comments made publicly and in writing (some of which are quoted), although not supported or condoned by enlightened thought. On the other hand, one cannot be sure that such perceptions do not still exist as long as there is truth to this sentence by B.H. Unruh: "Das Plattdeutsche gilt durchweg als eine minderwertige Sprache" (Low German is generally regarded as an inferior language).[35]

In about 1560, the Magdeburg Pastor Torquatus stated that High German had assumed such a predominant role, that the educated and those who have become educated through travel, write and speak Low German only with the greatest difficulty, and look with contempt upon those who speak it openly or privately.[36] In 1638 in Flensburg, the newly appointed General Superintendent (of the church) did away with the Low German language in church services, in place of which he imposed High German on the poor peasants.[37]

In 1794 the Pedagogue Gedike of Berlin guessed that in several more lifespans the Low German language would be dead to us.[38] In the magazine Pallas in 1801 appeared the statement, "Low German shall never be elevated to a book language. At the same time it is really an encumbrance to social culture."[39] In 1803, the magazine Hamburg und Altona boasted (without basis in fact), "Low German has been practically banished from superfine society, in fact the most humble pleb, without exception, not only understands High German, but either speaks it or is learning to speak it."[40] In 1924, Ziesemer stated, "In wide circles the attitude still prevails, even among the educated, that the language (dialect) of the people is of a lower rank, it is only the sunken language of the 'ordinary' people, from which one must keep one's distance."[41]

Although the eighteenth century is otherwise regarded as the century of enlightenment, of pietism, of knowledge of languages and of the pursuit of French cultural tastes, it was less than benevolent toward Low German. The zeal of people for education, and their dependence upon foreign tastes, not only clouded but degraded their perception of it. Such views culminated in the eighteenth century becoming the era of discrimination against the dialects, which Low German had by then become, because it was no longer written. It was perceived as a self-reproducing, space-bound, time-bound and socially-limited language of the lower stratum, from which the educationally-ambitious must hold themselves aloof. Even church pastors upheld this view, except perhaps at a wedding, when they might tolerate a Low German verse to be recited.[42]

Those views of Low German among the supposedly educated, probably engendered among its speakers many sayings, such as: "De Gelehrten sünd faken nich de Wiesen" (The learned are frequently not the wise).[43]

As related by Fritz Specht and others, there was one writer, apparently in the 19th century, who represents the "Judas" of Low German. He published an article entitled "Soll die plattdeutsche Sprache gepflegt oder ausgerottet werden? Gegen ersteres und für letzteres, beantwortet von Dr. Ludolf Wienbarg" (Should the Low German language be nurtured or rooted out? Opposed to the former and in favour of the latter, by Dr. Ludolf Wienbarg).

Paradoxically, the name "Wienbarg" is completely Low German. It means literally "wine hill" (vineyard). Had he wished to appropriate a degree of credibility for his outrageously contentious suggestion, he might have approached the public with his name in the altered form "Weinberg," which would be the High German form of Low German "Wienbarg."

Wienbarg went on in his German publication to say: "Low German is a stinking swamp, it can neither grasp nor transmit the intellectual and material progress of civilization. It thereby condemns a major portion of the North German population to minor (irresponsibility) status, to crudeness and to absence of idea, to exist in glaring contrast to the educated in the most revolting manner." "Whoever roots out Low German," he concludes, "earns himself a civic crown."[44]

In such atmosphere of negativism and discrimination, even among the "supposedly educated," as represented by the foregoing sampling, it is understandable that the changeover from Low German to High German was not without its agonies. It was certainly among the reasons why Low German ceased to be written and for centuries practically disappeared from the printed page.[45]

The Age of Spoken Low German. Nevertheless, during the several centuries that followed, Low German continued to be spoken by those same millions of people from the Netherlands to the Baltics who had always spoken it. Disdain for the Low German language and the cessation of the publication of quality Low German literature did not immediately diminish use of it among people at home and among friends. However, since interregional written communication and literature in Low German had ceased to exist, a period of dialectalization, beginning in the sixteenth century, eventually reduced the status of Low German to that of a dialect.

Dialectalization.[46] Dialectalization in this context means about the opposite of homogenization. It describes a degradation in the perception of a language from its status as a written language to one of an unwritten dialect. Dialectalization also means that homogeneity in a language is decreased, or that degradation of its cohensiveness decomposes it into dialects.

Just as homogenization in a language is fostered by closeness derived from active interchange of written information in business communications and/or in literature, so is dialectalization promoted by a reduction in written communication in a language. As the homogeneity of a language is encouraged by geographic proximity of people to each other, so is it reduced by the isolation of people from each other by distance or by other barriers.

When the Low German language went into decline in the sixteenth century, its speakers were spread from the Netherlands to the Baltic shores. When it ceased to be written, the bonding effects of active written business and literary communication were removed, and groups of speakers were left isolated from each other. Consequently, dialects in scattered regions grew apart from each other over the centuries because the written link fostering and preserving unity of the language no longer existed. Further to that, absence of it in writing eventually caused public perception of Low German to be degraded from that of a functional language to that of a dialect.

The result of centuries of dialectalization of Low German is that the Low German region of the North Sea and the Baltic Sea coastline of Europe now contains numerous dialects with pronounced differences among them, and no standardized Low German language. Among people world wide, many do not know that Low German is a language in its own right as opposed to being a dialect of German. Even among speakers of Low German, it is commonplace to encounter those with the opinion that Low German is an unwritten language.

The Reformation

Before the Reformation began in the sixteenth century, the High German language was already beginning to assume dominance in those areas of northern Germany where Low German had until then held sway. But, High German of that time still consisted of numerous dialects of German with pronounced variations among them, and without standardized form. Consequently, Martin Luther was faced with the problem of choosing a language from among those dialects for his translation of the Bible into German.

Today, it is not uncommon to hear the assertion that Luther's translation of the Bible into High German determined that it become the written and dominant language of all of Germany. However, it seems more evident that Luther wisely chose to join and support an already pervasive language movement. Progress of the Protestant Reformation in Germany was greatly enhanced by Luther choosing for his Bible a language by then already well on the way to becoming the standard written form and dominant language of Germany.[47] On the other hand, one cannot ignore that the personality and authority of the Reformer of Wittenberg, as Luther was known, rightly or wrongly earned him the reputation of being the creator of the High German written language. There can be no doubt that Luther was a major participant in shaping the final form of standardized High German.

When large segments of Germany were converted to Luther's New Gospel and joined the Lutheran Reformation, they were presented with the Gospel and the Bible in a new form of German, but one that most could understand. Until then, worship services had generally been conducted in Latin. Acceptance of the New Gospel and the language in which it was written came to be regarded as almost synonymous. Consequently, the High German text of the Luther Bible tended to be revered equally with the Divine Word. It came to be perceived as a sin against the spirit of Luther to use any language other than Luther's German for worship in a Lutheran church. Low German in worship was deemed to be incorrect, uncontrolled and deviant.[48]

Martin Luther grew up in a Low German neighborhood and well appreciated the Low German language.[49] He firmly believed that the New Gospel should be brought to the people in their own language. Therefore, one of Luther's personal friends and co-workers in the Reformation movement, Johannes Bugenhagen, together with a number of others at the University of Wittenberg undertook the translation of Luther's Bible into Low German. Scholars now disagree over criticisms of the Bugenhagen Bible as a failure in translation and an affront to Low German.[50] However, all agree that Low German literature cannot be created by substituting Low German words for those in a passage of High German literature. Bugenhagen's translators attempted that—and failed.

Luther encouraged the placement of Low German pastors in Low German communities.[51] But he could not overcome the shortage of Low German pastors for northern congregations. Protestant northern Germany had only three universities. In all of northwest Germany there was not a single theological training institute.[52] The lack of theological training in Low German northwestern Germany unavoidably contributed to a trend to fill northern pastoral openings with men who had been trained elsewhere. The inevitable result was that men who had trained in southern High German universities became pastors of northern Low German Lutheran congregations.[53]

Young men of the north who wished to train for the ministry usually studied in Wittenberg. When they returned to their local northern congregations, they had been trained in High German which they then used in worship services to replace the former Latin.[54] Northern congregations protested to church authorities that they could not understand the High German spoken by their pastors, but the authorities could not or did not change, and the protests had no particular effect.

The reaction among Low German congregations was to adjust to the inevitable and to let "those up there" speak and write as they would—most couldn't read it in any event. But, when people spoke, sang and prayed outside the church, they continued to do so in the local Low German language.[55] Low German Bibles, prayer books and catechisms continued to appear as late as the mid-eighteenth century, but without particular appreciation by church officials.[56]

Summary of Chapter Three

The Early Period of the Middle Low German period is not represented by surviving literature. The Classical part of the period was the time during which Low German became the leading language of northern Europe. It was then the language of business and diplomacy, used in the offices of the Hanseatic League which dominated trade and international affairs from London to Memel and from Brügge to Novgorod. The Late Period marks the decline in use of Low German subsequent to the failure of the Hanseatic League.

The decline and demise of the Hanseatic League in the sixteenth century cast a pall upon the Low German language that brought about its rejection, practically wiping it from the printed page by the late 1500's.

After failure of the League, its former business enterprises were taken over by merchants of England, Holland and southern Germany. The language of business, as well as all other activities in Germany, thereafter gradually became High German.

Luther joined this trend for change and wrote his translation of the Bible for German people in the incoming High German. The vocabulary he chose and used in his Bible translation was taken from among different German dialects, including also some Low German. The choices he made among them, in large measure determined the character of the official standard German of today.

Today, the national language of Germany is High German, even in those areas that were formerly and traditionally Low German.

NOTES TO CHAPTER THREE

Note: See Notes to Chapter One for Abbreviations

1. The word "Middle" in this case is not to be interpreted as having a geographic connotation as in "middle" Europe. It relates to time in history as in "Middle Ages."

2. Dieter Stellmacher, *Niederdeutsche Sprache,* Langs Germanistische Lehrbuchsammlung, Band 26, (Bern: Verlag Peter Lang AG, 1990), p. 39.

3. *Ibid.*, p. 39.

4. *Encyclopædia Britannica*, "Hanseatic League," (Chicago: William Benton, Publisher, 1959), Vol. 11, p. 162b.

5. *Encycl. Brit.*, "Teutonic Order, The," 1959, Vol. 21, pp. 983a-984.

6. *Encycl. Brit.*, "Hanseatic League," 1959, Vol.11, p. 164.

7. Claus Schuppenhauer, *Niederdeutsch Heute*, (Leer: Verlag Schuster Leer, 1976), p. 5.
—Artur Gabrielsson, "Die Verdrangung der mittelniederdeutschen Sprache," *Handbuch zur niederdeutschen Sprach-und Literaturwissenschaft*, (Berlin: Erich Schmidt Verlag, 1983), p. 119.

8. Karl Bischoff, "Mittelniederdeutsch," *NSL*, pp. 105-108.

9. *Ibid.*, pp. 111-112.

10. *Ibid.*, p. 99.

11. *Ibid.*, p. 108.

12. Artur Gabrielsson, "Die Verdrängung der mittelniederdeutschen Sprache", *NSL*, pp. 119-120.

13. Artur Gabrielsson, "Die Verdrängung der mittelniederdeutsche Sprache", *NSL*, p. 131 .

14. Encycl. Brit., "Gotland", 1959, Vol. 10, p. 553a.

15. Artur Gabrielsson, "Die Verdrangung der mittelniederdeutschen Sprache", *NSL*, p. 131.
    —Encycl. Brit., "Denmark", 1959, Vol. 7, p. 205b.

16. *Encycl. Brit.*, "Hanseatic League", 1959, Vol. 11, p. 164d.

17. Karl Hyldgaard-Jensen, "Mittelniederdeutsch und die skandinavischen Sprachen", *NSL*, p. 675.

18. Artur Gabrielsson, "Die Verdrangung der mnd. Sprache", *NSL*, p. 123.

19. *Ibid.*, p. 120.

20. *Ibid.*, p. 120-121.

21. *Encycl. Brit.*, "John Cabot," 1959, Vol. 4, 507a. Cabot, as governor of the Company of Merchant Adventurers of England, discovered the sea route into northern Russia via the White Sea and the (northern) Dvina in 1553. He made his way overland to Moscow, opening up a very considerable trade with England.

22. Artur Gabrielsson, "Die Verdrängung der mnd. Sprache", *NSL*, p. 121.

23. *Ibid.*, p. 122.

24. *Ibid.*, p. 122.

25. *Ibid.*, p. 124.

26. *Ibid.*, p. 125.

27. *Ibid.*, p. 129.

28. Stellmacher, *NS*, p. 69.

29. *Ibid.*, p. 71.

30. Ulf Bichel, "Drama", *NSL*, p. 392.

31. Artur Gabrielsson, "Die Verdrängung der mnd. Sprache", *NSL*, p. 137.

32. *Ibid.*, p. 131.

33. *Ibid.*, pp. 132-133.

34. *Ibid.*, p. 135.

35. Unruh, p. 16.

36. Karl Bischoff, "Mittelniederdeutsch", *NSL*, p. 115.

37. Artur Gabrielsson, "Die Verdrängung der mnd. Sprache", *NSL*, p. 144.

38. Dieter Möhn, "Geschichte der nnd. Mundarten", *NSL*, p. 154.

39. *Ibid.*, p. 155.

40. *Ibid.*, p. 159.

41. Walther Ziesemer, *Die Ostpreussischen Mundarten*, (Wiesbaden: Dr. Martin Sandig oHG., 1970) Vorwort, p. III.

42. Johann Dietrich Bellmann, "Niederdeutsch als Kirchensprache", *NSL*, p. 618.

43. Claus Schuppenhauer, *Niederdeutsch Heute*, p. 49.

44. Fritz Specht, *Plattdeutsch wie es nicht im Worterbuch steht*, (Frankfurt: Verlag Heinrich Scheffler, 1969), p. 186.

45. Dieter Möhn, "Geschichte der nnd. Mundarten", *NSL*, p. 165.

46. Stellmacher, *NS*, p. 69.

47. Artur Gabrielsson, "Die Verdrängung der mnd. Sprache", *NSL*, p. 136.

48. Artur Gabrielsson, "Die Verdrängung der mnd. Sprache", *NSL*, p. 136.
    —Dieter Stellmacher, *Niederdeutsche Sprache*, p. 72.

49. Stellmacher, *Niederdeutsche Sprache*, p. 73.

50. Johann Dietrich Bellmann, "Niederdeutsch als Kirchensprache", *NSL*, p. 614.
—Stellmacher, *Niederdeutsche Sprache*, p. 74.

51. Karl Bischoff, "Mittelniederdeutsch", *NSL*, p. 116.

52. Johann Diedrich Bellmann, "Niederdeutsch als Kirchensprache", *NSL*, p. 616.

53. *Ibid.*, p. 616.

54. *Ibid.*, p. 616.

55. *Ibid.*, p. 617.

56. *Ibid.*, p. 617.
—Stellmacher, *Niederdeutsche Sprache*, p. 72.

CHAPTER FOUR

The History of Low German—Part III

The Modern Low German Period

Social attitudes engendered by the failure of the Hanseatic League shifted public admiration from Low German to High German. A mounting disrespect for Low German eventually drove it out of print. It subsequently remained unwritten and disdained as a lower-class peasant language for almost three centuries. It would not have seemed surprising if the language had died out entirely at that time. But, that did not happen. In fact, far from it. Today, Low German is spoken by millions of people in Germany and elsewhere. The fact that it is very much alive is proclaimed by author Karl Fissen in his book entitled: "Plattdütsch läwt!" (Low German lives!).[1]

One might wonder how it came about that millions of Germans continue to speak Low German after their language lost its status several centuries ago. It cannot be denied that Low German people had the High German language imposed upon them. They were coerced by intimidating circumstances to learn to speak, read and write it as a strange second language which they were then expected to use in public, in business and possibly at work. However, such coercion could not reach people in their homes; it could not compel them to give up their mother tongue in the intimate surroundings of home and friends. To do so would have been as impossible then as it has been under totalitarian governments since.

Those Low German people who were at that time employed in the business world, where the adopted use of High German was necessary in order to succeed, still regarded the home as the warm nest where one could relax in a cosy, familiar atmosphere. In the company of family and friends, one could talk in the old familiar manner, in comfort and at ease, and one could express without reservation and understandably, those feelings that sprang from the heart.

The Low German language embodies certain unique, life-sustaining qualities that seem to evade precise description. In this regard, it seems different from other languages. These qualities have contributed to its preservation among people who inherited it as their mother tongue.

Those on the land seldom came into contact with "officialdom." They lived their lives in rural communities where conversation and discussion continued in Low German. For "official" matters one would travel to the nearest town and seek out an official known for his ability to handle such matters in High German, but who would discuss them in Low German. This continues to this day.

"Niederdeutsch Heute"[2] (Low German Today) of 1976 presents the views of various authors, businesspeople, educators and public officials on their personal experiences with Low German, describing its perceived characteristics. A consensus among those lengthy descriptions is here condensed into English phrases, as follows:

A harmonizing effect on conversation; brings people together more easily; ameliorates interhuman difficulties; bridges social differences; embodies capabilities for expression overshadowing those of High German; holds literary treasures seldom found elsewhere; uniquely expresses humor, relieves tension and expresses joy; a soft hand stroking the heart; a bridge from one to the other; goes over no one's head; its intimacy dissolves harshness; is robust without being brusque; its lack of abrasiveness promotes "Gelassenheit" (composure) and "Gemütlichkeit" (comfort).[3]

RENAISSANCE IN LOW GERMAN LITERATURE

The Low German language continued to be spoken by millions of people in northern Germany throughout the centuries following the ending of the Middle Low German Period in about 1650. The Modern Low German Period is considered to have begun in about 1850. At the end of the Middle Low German Period the language disappeared from the written page, although literature of quality had not been published since the late 1500's. The beginning of the Modern Low German Period is marked by the time when Low German literature again began to be published.

Today, it is difficult to understand how or why the publication of Low German literature should once more begin in the 1850's. But, as the eighteenth century was the century of discrimination against the dialects, so the nineteenth century was a century of sociological change resulting from the industrial revolution. Just how those changes then affected Low German literature cannot now be fully appreciated.

The collapse of the Hanseatic League brought about social change that created negative attitudes toward Low German. The result of those attitudes was the disappearance of Low German literature. Then, some three centuries later, came the industrial revolution with far-reaching sociological changes and positive influences upon social outlook and literary awareness that reversed those negative attitudes. That scene caught the attentions of Johann Peter Hebel and Klaus Groth.

Those potential wordsmiths recognized that the times were opportune

34

to withdraw from the forge of history those irons that had reached ready malleability after decades in the glowing coals of social change. They took them and shaped them on the anvil of the nineteenth century into the literary forms then awaited by a society with altered attitudes. The parts played by those writers in the course of language development for that period cannot be regarded as mere historical accident.[4]

When Hebel published a book of dialect verse entitled "Alemannischen Gedichten" in 1803, he proved that the public attitudes that confined dialect literature for centuries had finally relented enough to be overcome. Fifty years later, when Groth published his "Quickborn" (Bubbling Spring) in the Low German dialect of Schleswig-Holstein, he also demonstrated that the dyke was indeed broken.

Groth's breakthrough in Low German ushered in a renaissance in Low German literature that continues unabated until today.[5] Hertell[6] states that the re-emergence of dialect literature in the nineteenth century was engendered by increased literary consciousness resulting from social revolution.

Klaus Groth. Klaus Groth's original publication of Quickborn (Bubbling Spring) was followed in quick succession by seven expanded and rewritten editions between 1852 and 1857, all of which found ready acceptance and set the tone for further publications in Low German by others.

Fritz Reuter. In 1853, Fritz Reuter ventured onto the scene with his "Läuschen un Riemels" (Verses and Rhymes) written in the Low German dialect of Mecklenburg. Although his verses were not of outstanding lyrical quality, they were nevertheless well received. Reuter went on to become a prolific, successful and highly-admired author of Low German whose masterpiece was a gripping socio-critical poem entitled "Kein Hüsung" (No Housing), of over four thousand lines.

John Brinckman. Then in 1859, Reuter's contemporary and fellow Mecklenburger, John Brinckman, entered the literary scene with a book of verse entitled "Vagel Grip" (Bird trap), reminiscent of his home town of Rostock. Both Reuter and Brinckman subtly and scathingly ridiculed the naivety of the pro-High-German-con-Low-German attitude still much in vogue in some quarters, and the Low-German-cum-High-German "Missingsch" (amalgam) dialect that it engendered. One of Brinckman's greatest works is "Dei General-Reeder" (The Chief Shipper), an engaging story of more than forty printed pages, of life and faith in the seafaring tradition of his people.

Literature. Once resistance to publishing in Low German had faded, and the aforementioned authors had tested the waters and found them inviting, the tide of Low German literature rose and has continued to rise with few interruptions in quantity and quality until this day. It spread across the Low German north. Authors sprang up in most dialectical areas. Among the areas that, for unexplained reasons, were not proportionately represented in this literary resurgence, was Prussia.[7] In

Prussia, the Nether Prussian dialects of the Nether Saxon family of dialects, were spoken. They included Mennonite Plautdietsch.

Characteristics of Nether Saxon Low German

As mentioned in previous chapters, Nether Saxon Low German exists in numerous dialects but without an overall standard form. Some of the differences between dialects are so great as to create difficulties for a speaker of one to understand a speaker of another. In other cases the differences are less pronounced. Each region has peculiarities of speech common to the dialects within that region. The characteristics common to the several dialects of one region may be different from characteristics peculiar to dialects of another neighboring region.

EASTERN AND WESTERN
LOW GERMAN

Such differences in general characteristics are found between eastern and western sections of the Low German language zone in Germany, which is therefore divided into an Eastern Low German region (Ostniederdeutsch) and a Western Low German region (Westniederdeutsch), (Map #3, p. 37). The distinctions between East and West are mainly grammatical and pronunciational characteristics of speech in each region. A group of dialects at the northeastern end of the Eastern Low German region is called Niederpreußisch (Nether Prussian), but is/was[8] in fact part of Ostniederdeutsch (Eastern Low German).

Verb endings "en" and "t". One of the more noticeable differences in the spoken word in the eastern and western Low German language regions lies in their different verb endings in the Present Indicative, plural, first, second and third persons. In order to make a simple, easy-to-understand east-west comparison, let us compare English and German plus eastern and western Low German versions of the following simple statement:

we/you/they: "make" or "sing"

English   **German**
1. we make (sing)   wir machen (singen)
2. you make (sing)   ihr macht (singt)
3. they make (sing)   sie machen (singen)

Note that in English, as in these examples, the verb does not change its form or suffix in the three persons plural. This grammatical construction is similar to that of Low German. German verbs, however, change their form between persons, ending with "en" in the first and third persons plural, but ending with "t" in the second person plural. The above examples follow the general rule for English and German verbs in this context.

36

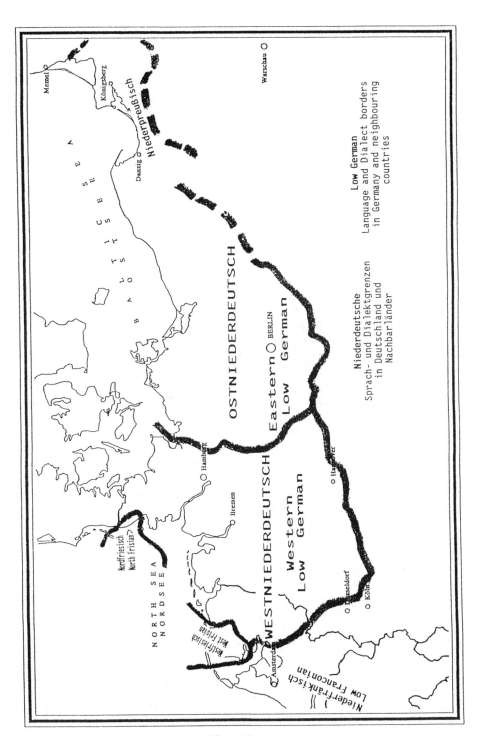

Map #3

Eastern Low German	Western Low German
(Ostniederdeutsch)	(Westniederdeutsch)
1. wi maken (singen)	wi makt (singt)
2. ji maken (singen)	ji makt (singt)
3. se maken (singen)	se makt (singt)

As seen in the foregoing examples, Low German verbs in this context retain the same form in all three persons plural, but a distinct difference prevails between verb suffixes for East and West. Eastern verbs in this context end with "en", whereas western verbs end with "et" or "t" (except as noted below).

When we compare these usages with English and German, we see that the Low German verbs remain unchanged in all three plural persons, as do those in English. On the other hand, while the "en" endings in eastern Low German are similar to first and third person plurals in German, the "t" endings of western Low German emulate the German second person plural form.

Since speakers of Low German in East and West Germany are sensitive to these verb endings,[9] an important thing to remember about their uses there is that in the East one must say "wi maken" and "wi singen" whereas in the West one says "wi makt" and "wi singt."

However, as happens in languages, especially those spoken in a large region, there are areas within the western Low German region where application of the "t" suffix rule for verbs does not uniformly apply. In parts of East Friesland and the Netherlands, as well as in a northern portion of Schleswig-Holstein (Map #4, p. 39), the plural verb endings follow the eastern "en" pattern.[10] The reason for this exception to western pattern in these small regions is not clear.[11]

What appears to be yet another exception in Nether Prussian dialects is actually only a pronunciational difference in that the "n" of the "en" verb endings is usually muted or not spoken. In most dialects of Nether Prussian, the verbs "maken" and "singen" become "make" and "singe", with the final "e" spoken as a schwa.

Initial "ss" and "sch". An example of Low German pronunciations in a portion of the eastern region is illustrated by Specht[12] in the following sentence: "Schnied mi mal'n Schned Schwattbrot af" (cut me [once] a slice of darkbread [off]), which is abhorrent to western Low German ears because the initial "sch" smacks of High German. In much of western Low German the "sch" becomes "ss", as in "Ssnied", "Ssned" and "Sswattbrot." In Mennonite Plautdietsch, an eastern dialect, it reads: "Schnied mi mol 'ne Schnäd Schwoatbroot auf." (Note that German "sch" is pronounced the same as English "sh").

Dative and Accusative Cases. Since no standardized form exists for Low German, no officially correct grammar exists for it. As might be expected, this has led to differences in application of dative or accusative cases to articles and pronouns. In English the dative case is not recognized.[13] In German the cases are meticulously observed. In Low German

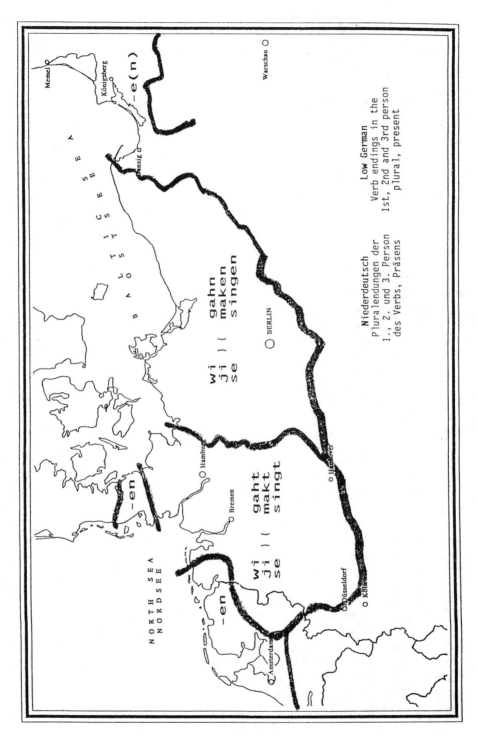

Map #4

no difference is generally made between dative and accusative cases, but wording in one region may seem to indicate the accusative case, whereas in another area the dative seems to prevail.

In western Low German, one would say "an den Tun"[14] for (on the fence), which sounds like the accusative case to the High German ear. In the East, this would be said: "an dem Tun", which sounds dative. In Plautdietsch, one says: "aun däm Tun" or simply "aum Tun," although some, especially those who are familiar with High German grammar, might say "aun den Tun." Little further attention is given to accusative and dative in Low German. Such laxity would be intolerable in High German.

For someone like this writer, born in Canada of Low German parents who never spoke with their children in High German, having learned English (in which the dative case is not recognized) and Low German (in which dative and accusative are not clearly defined), the ear is untuned for German grammar. In High German, one must carefully distinguish and identify the cases when selecting appropriate endings for articles before nouns.

The difference between dative and accusative cases can be simply illustrated in the following English sentences: "He gives me it" and "He hits me." In the first sentence, one actually says: "He gives it (to) me." In this sentence, "it" is the direct object of "gives" (accusative case), whereas "me" following (to) is the indirect object (dative case).

In the second sentence: "He hits me," there can be little doubt that "me" is the direct object of "hits." Therefore, "me" is in the accusative case. In English it is correct to use the pronoun "me" in both cases, as is also true in Low German where it is spelled "mi." But, in High German the dative form of "me" is "mir," the accusative form is "mich."

The misuse or misplacement of pronouns "mir" and "mich" or articles "dem" and "den," by those who have grown up with Low German and then attempt High German, has led to many humorous anecdotes and jests. On the other hand, it is equally humorous when the speaker of Low German, having subsequently also mastered the grammar of High German, then sets out to put the Low German house in order, so to speak, by applying proper High German grammar to it. It simply does not work!

Low German Vowels

It has been observed of Low German that most of the dialects do not favour simple vowels, but tend to make them into diphthongs.[15] Actually, in some dialects diphthongs and triphthongs are more common than simple vowels, and occasionally they extend into quadriphthongs, as for example: "Heiaust" (haying time). The following examples are representative of Low German diphthong enunciations which are not necessarily common to all dialects.

The long "o" in Low German usually becomes a diphthong, ending with a "u." A Low German word embodying this diphthong is the word for "good," which is usually written "goot", but is pronounced "goᵘt." Its Low German pronunciation is midway between "goat" and "gout" in English.

The long High German "e," written "ee" (pronounced as English "ay" in "day") usually becomes a diphthong in Low German, ending with a short, diminished "i" (pronounced "eeⁱ" or English "ayⁱ"). The word for English "Sea" is written "See" in both High German and Low German. In German it is pronounced "zay" (as in English "zany") whereas in Low German it is pronounced "zayⁱ", with diminished emphasis on the "i." The Low German "ee" is a diphthong, but similar to the "ei" in the English word "beige". In Low German one might write Sea as "Seei", but it is usually written "See."

Of these pronunciational peculiarities, Specht[16] says, "Ja, ja, dat geiht narns bunter to as op de Welt" (Yes, yes, it happens nowhere more colorfully than on this earth).

English and Low German Words (Identical or Similar)

The common roots of English and Low German are evident in that many Old Saxon words exist in both languages. Due to changes that take place in a language over time, some Old Saxon words in English and Low German have become unrecognizable in their current spoken forms. Others have not changed much, or else changes have been minor and similar. In such cases the Saxon words are still similar in both languages fifteen centuries after the Saxons of Britain and those of the continent went their separate ways.

The following table lists in modern form some of those English and Low German words that stem directly from the Old Saxon language. Those Old Saxon words that are common to both languages, but which have lost their similarity in form, are not shown. Words assimilated into both languages after the Old Saxon period, or from other languages such as Latin or French, are also not included. All the words listed meet the following requirements:

    a. They derive directly from Old Saxon words as confirmed by "The Oxford Dictionary of English Etymology."

    b. Their modern forms are of the same meaning and are identical or recognizably similar in their English and Low German forms.

    c. They are identical or similar in the Low German language in general as well as in the Plautdietsch dialect in particular.

    d. Low German (general) words are from "Plattdeutsches Wörterbuch" by Wolfgang Lindow (1984), which covers numerous dialects.

    e. Plautdietsch words are from dictionaries by Herman Rempel, Jack Thiessen, or as known to this writer.

41

English	Low German (Language in general)	Plautdietsch (Dialect in particular)
above	baben, baven boben	bowe(n)
alone	alleen, allein	auleen
arm	Arm	Oarm
ash	Asch	Ausch
babble	babbeln	bauble(n)
bake	backen	backe(n)
band	Band	Baund
beard	Baart, Bort Bart	Boat
bed	Bett, Bedd Berr	Bad
better	beter, bäter better	bäta
bid	bidden	beede(n) bedde(n)
bind	binnen, binden	binje(n)
bite	bieten	biete(n)
blind	blind	blind
bloom	Bloom	Bloom
blossoms	Blössem	Blassem
boat	Boot	Boot
book	Book	Buak
boss	Baas, Boos	Bauss
brake	breken	bräakje(n)
bridge	Brüch, Brügg Brück	Brigj
bring	bringen	brinje(n)
buck	Bock, Buck	Bock
butter	Botter	Botta
calf	Kalf	Kaulf
claw	Klau, Klaw	Klau, Kleiw
clock	Klock	Klock
cold	koolt, koold kolt	kolt
come	kamen, komen	kome(n)
cook	kaken, koken	koake(n)
dam	Damm	Daum
dance	danzen, dansen	daunze(n)
day	Dag, Dach	Dag,Dach
deep	deep	deep
do	doon	doone(n)
door	Döör	Däa

drink	drinken	drinkje(n)
drive	drieben, driven	driewe(n)
	drieven	
dumb	dumm	domm
earnest	eernst, ernst	earnst, iernst
	irnst	
earth	Eerd, Eert,	Ead
	Ierd	
eat	eten, etten	äte(n)
end	End, Enn	Enj
fall	fallen	faule(n)
fast	fast, fass	faust
father	Vadder, Vader	Voda
fever	Fever, Fewer	Feeba
	Feber	
file	Fiel, Fill	Fiel
find	finden, finnen	finje(n)
finger	Finger	Finja
fire	Füer, Füür	Fia
fish	Fisch, Fisk	Fesch
flesh	Fleesch	Fleesch
flood	Floot	Floot
fly	flegen, fleigen	flieeje(n),
		fleeje(n)
		fläje(n)
foot	Faut, Foot	Foot
fore	vör, vöör, vor	vää
foul	ful, fuul	ful
fox	Voss	Voss
free	fre, frie	frie
fresh	frisch	fresch
friend	Frönd, Fründ	Frind
frost	Frost, Fröst	Frost
full	voll, vull	voll
gall	Gall	Gaul
gander	Ganner, Ganter	Gaunta
	Genner	
give	geben, geven	jäwe(n)
glass	Glas	Glaus
glide	glieden	jliede(n)
go	gahn, gohn	gohne(n)
good	gaud, good	goot
	goot, guud	
grass	Gras	Graus
grave	Graff, Graft	Grauf
guest	Gast	Gaust

43

halter	Halter	Haulta
hammer	Hamer, Hammer Hom(m)er	Homa
hand	Hand	Haund
hard	hart, hatt	hoat
harvest	Har(v)st, Harfs Harss	Hoawst
he	he, hei	he
hear	hören, hüren	heare(n)
help	helpen, hölpen	halpe(n)
honey	Honnig	Honnig
hoof	Hauf, Hoof	Hoof
horn	Hoorn, Horn Hurn	Huarn
hound	Hund	Hund
house	Huus	Hus
hunger	Hunger	Hunga
ice	Ies	Ies
is	is	es
it	et	et
kettle	Kätel, Ketel	Kjätel
knead	knäden, knede	kjnäde(n)
knee	Knee, Knei	Kjnee
land	Land	Laund
late	laat, lat	lot
laugh	lachen	lache(n)
let	laten	lote(n)
lick	licken	leckje(n)
lie	legen, leigen lögen	lieeje(n) leeje(n) läje(n)
light	Licht, Liecht	Licht
long	lang	lang
loud	luud, luut	lud
lung	Lung	Lung
make	maken	moake(n)
man	Mann	Maun
milk	Melk, Mölk	Malkj
mother	Moder, Mudder	Mutta
mud	Maad, Modder Mudd, Mudder	Modd
nail	Nagel	Noagel
naked	naakt, nakelt	noakendig, noaktig
name	Naam	Nome
neighbour	Naber, Nawer Nober	Noba

44

north	noorden, norden	nuade(n)
nose	Nääs, Nees	Näs
oak	Eek, Eik, Eker	Eakj
old	old, olt	oolt
open	apen, open	op
out	ut, uut	ut
over	öber, över, over	äwa
ox	Oss	Oss
pepper	Peper	Päpa
rain	rägen, regen	räajne(n)
rib	Ribb, Ripp	Rebb
room	ruum	rum, ruum
rudder	Rauder, Roder Roor	Ruda
run	rönnen	rane(n)
rust	Rust	Rost
salt	Sult	Solt
sand	Sand	Saund
sea	See, Sei	See
seek	säuken, söken	seakje(n)
sharp	scharp	schoap
ship	Schipp	Schepp
shoe	Schauh, Schoh	Schooh
shudder	schudern, schuddern	schudere(n) schuddere(n)
side	Sied, Siet	Sied
sister	Süster	Sesta
sit	sitten	sette(n)
sour	suer, suur	sua
spring	springen	sprinje(n)
still	still	stell
summer	Sommer, Sömmer Summer, Sümmer	Somma
swear	sweren, swören	schweare(n)
sweat	Sweet, Sweit	Schweet
swim	swemmen swömmen, swümmen	schwame(n)
swine	Swien	Schwien
that	dat	daut
thaw	dauen,	deiwe(n), daue(n)
the	de	de
thick	dick	dickj
thistle	Distel, Diessel	Distel

three	dree, drei	dree
tongue	Tung	Tung
true	tro, tru	tru
twelve	twölf, twolf	twalf, twalw
under	ünner	unja
up	op, up	opp
warm	warm	woarm
wash	waschen	wausche(n)
water	Water, Woter	Wota
weather	Wedder, Weer	Wada
	Weller, Werrer	
wild	wild	wild
will	willen, wullen	welle(n)
	wüllen	
wind	Wind	Wind
wind (to)	winden, winnen	winje(n)
winter	Winter	Winta
word	Woord, Woort	Wuat
	Wuurt	
work	Wark	Woakj
wring	wringen	wrinje(n)
young	jung	jung

Summary of Chapter Four

The collapse of the Hanseatic League in the sixteenth century generated attitudes toward Low German that forced it from the printed page. The Industrial Revolution brought about social change that enhanced people's perceptions of dialect literature. This fostered a "Renaissance" in Low German literature that shows no signs of abating. Since mid-nineteenth century, Low German has produced a continuum of dialect literature, unmatched in volume and content by any other language. Schuppenhauer concludes that people's love for Low German and their tenacity in clinging to it appear to spring from man's basic motives for existence.[17]

Characteristic grammatical differences between eastern and western Low German are "en" and "et" verb endings as in "wi singen" in eastern Low German, and "wi singt" in western. Pronunciational differences may occur in initial "ss" or "sch," such as "schnacken" in eastern Low German as compared to "ssnacken" in western. Laxity in distinuishing between dative and accusative cases in Low German is reminiscent of the lack of observance of the dative in English. What comes out as dative in one Low German region may appear as accusative in another. This contrasts sharply with strict observance of cases in German.

Some of the many Old Saxon words common to English and Low German are shown in a listing of some 173 modern English words and their Low German equivalents. English words in column one are matched with their identical or similar Low German counterparts in column two. Low German words are from a 1984 dictionary published by the "Institut für niederdeutsche Sprache" (Institute for the Low German language) in Bremen which lists words in numerous, but not all, dialects of the language. Column three lists the equivalent words as they appear in the Mennonite dialect of Low German known as Plautdietsch.

Although 173 English words are indeed a small sampling, the uniformities and obvious relationships between these few and their Low German equivalents illustrate the postulated relationship between the two languages: The Low German and English languages descend directly from a common Old Saxon mother language which was carried to Britain from the Netherlands and northern Germany about fifteen centuries ago. Consequently, English and Low German are sister languages, Low German being the older sister.

NOTES TO CHAPTER FOUR

Note: See Notes to Chapter One for Abbreviations

1. Karl Fissen, *Plattdütsch lawt!,* (Oldenburg: Heinz Holzberg Verlag, 1963).

2. Claus Schuppenhauer, *Niederdeutsch Heute,* Institut für niederdeutsche Sprache, (Leer: Verlag Schuster Leer, 1976).

3. *Ibid.*

4. *Ibid.,* p. 419.

5. *Ibid.,* pp. 418-433.

6. Jörg Eiben-von Hertell, "Lyric", *NSL,* p. 419.

7. Ulrich Tolksdorf, "Die Mundartliteratur Westpreußens," *Der Westpreuße,* (4400 Munster, Norbertstraße 29, 1991) p. 65.

8. The dialects referred to as Nether Prussian (Niederpreußisch) were those of East and West Prussia whose inhabitants were driven out in 1945. All of Prussia officially ceased to exist, by allied agreement, shortly thereafter. Those who escaped with their lives may still be speaking Nether Prussian, but not in Prussia.

9. Fritz Specht, *Plattdeutsch wie es nicht im Worterbuch steht,* (Frankfurt: Verlag Heinrich Scheffler, 1969), p. 14.
   —Dieter Stellmacher, Niederdeutsche Sprache, Langs Germanistische Lehrbuchsammlung, Band 26, (Bern: Verlag Peter Lang AG, 1990), pp. 146, 149.
   —Dieter Stellmacher, "Phonologie und Morphologie", *NSL,* p. 240.

10. Dieter Stellmacher, "Phonologie und Morphologie", *NSL,* p. 268.

11. Karl Bischoff, "Mittelniederdeutsch", *NSL,* p. 113. Bischoff states that the presence of 'en' plural verb endings in East Friesland, where one would expect the western 't' verb suffix to prevail, is probably a holdover from the time when eastern Low German of the Hanseatic League must have been extensively spoken, and that its spoken form played a role when the Frisian language was displaced by Nether Saxon Low German in East Friesland. Although such theory might explain the existence of eastern speech characteristics in the vicinity of major western Hanseatic trading centres such as Emden in East Friesland or Brügge in Flanders, it is unclear how this would explain a similar 'en' verb suffix zone in northern Schlewig-Holstein, near the border with Denmark.

12. Fritz Specht, *Plattdeutsch wie es nicht im Worterbuch steht,* (Frankfurt: Verlag Heinrich Scheffler, 1969), p. 14.

13. Donald O. Bolander, *Practical English,* (Chicago: Career Institute, 1961), Vol. 1, p. 9:05.

14. Specht, p. 15.

15. *Ibid.*, p. 15.

16. *Ibid.*, p. 15.

17. Claus Schuppenhauer, *Niederdeutsch Heute,* Institut fur niederdeutsche Sprache, (Leer: Verlag Schuster Leer, 1976), p. 6.

CHAPTER FIVE

The Origins of the Netherlandic Mennonites and their Language

The Frisian Homeland,
Frisia Triplex

The Frisian people, whose name in Gothic means "The Free Ones," are known in early history as the people who occupied the islands and North Sea coast of what we now know as the Netherlands and Germany. Their meagre livelihood on the low-lying coastal marshlands was continually threatened and attacked over the centuries by their two chief enemies: the sea and the Normans. Since the coastline of Friesland was gradually sinking for geological reasons, engulfment by the sea was a continual and growing threat, against which they energetically, though often futilely, strove to defend themselves. Until the beginning of the eleventh century, piratical raids upon them by the Normans laid waste their farmlands, homes and villages and took many of them to be sold into slavery. Although their story reads as a tragedy, it is noted that centuries of efforts to defend themselves against the sea and against attack from their enemies left them with a reputation for which they became known as "Gottes Ehrenvolk" (God's people of honour).[1]

The Romans had reported of the Frisians that they were a people exceeding all others in courage and loyalty. The English monk Bartholomaeus Anglicus wrote of them as being strong, proud of their freedom and peculiar customs. They had earned a reputation among other peoples of being "rough and free".

Their pride prompted their heroes to reject offers of knighthood because, as they claimed, they were all knights already.[2] In 1555, Philip of Spain accepted the oath of allegiance from all provinces of the Netherlands. All delegates went to their knees before him, except the Frisians, who remained standing with the explanation, "De Friesen knielje alline foar God!" (The Frisians kneel only before God!).[3]

One of the characteristics of the Frisian nature for which they became known was their persistent feuding among themselves. They carried on their internal feuds with intensity, interrupting them only when attack

49

by a common enemy forced them to desist and to band together. Unruh points out the parallel between such feuds and schisms among Mennonite descendants of Frisians.[4]

The Frisians courageously defended their freedom from all outsiders who attempted to bring them under subjection, even the neighboring provinces of Holland (The West Frisians killed William, Count of Holland in 1256).[5] Even during those times when their independence was severely threatened by superior force, they maintained their sovereign rights and distinctiveness of nationality and language.[6]

Frisian Refuge. In the sixteenth century, the Frisian people inhabited the greater Friesland consisting of West Friesland, Groningen and East Friesland, also known as the Frisia Triplex (Map #1, p. 7).[7] The characteristic independence of the Frisians shielded their homeland somewhat from the intruding reach of outside authority. In addition, the relatively inaccessible expanses of marshlands of the low-lying coastal areas of the Netherlands along the North Sea enhanced the Frisia Triplex as a haven from oppressors. Frisia also provided a route of escape by sea or overland to the East, should that become necessary.

During the Reformation, many of those dissatisfied with existing religious institutions, reformed and otherwise, embraced "nonconformist" religious teachings. Nonconformity quite often, almost regularly, led to persistent and cruel suppression and retaliation against such dissenters by religious and administrative authorities.[8] Whole families of them, mostly sincere Christians whose faiths differed from those of established churches, were forced to flee for their lives. Those who failed to escape, frequently died the deaths of martyrs. Many of them sought refuge in the northern parts of the Netherlands, especially among the Frisians, among whom at one time one quarter were Anabaptists,[9] one of the dissenting factions.

During the first half of the sixteenth century there was a great increase in the number of Anabaptists gathered in the Frisia Triplex and in the neighboring provinces of the Netherlands and Germany. Until then, this small area of Europe had escaped much of the intense pursuit of religious dissidents carried out elsewhere. This changed as the Counter Reformation continued and the powers of governments shifted.

The Peaceful Anabaptists. So, it came about that the Netherlands and northern Germany became a haven for great numbers of "Anabaptists" of various stripe, including some who proposed to establish God's kingdom through violent overthrow of government, and others who believed that Christ was the Prince of Peace. The Anabaptists of the Frisia Triplex at that time, consisting in the main of local Frisians whose ranks had been swelled by incoming Flemish Anabaptist refugees from Flanders as well as some from southern Germany, were mostly of peaceful orientation.

Menno Simons. In 1536, in the village of Witmarsum in West Friesland, a Frisian Roman Catholic priest by the name of Menno Simons who, having studied the Bible, became convinced of the cause of the peaceful Anabaptists. He gave up the Roman priesthood, was baptized by local Anabaptists, and within a short time became their dedicated elder and leader.[10]

The Münsterites. Only a year or two earlier, in 1534-1535, a violent and disastrous insurrection by Anabaptists in the German city of Münster[11] ended in a massacre. This had given the whole movement a reputation from which the peaceful Anabaptists in the Frisia Triplex had good reason to wish to distance themselves. The Münsterite rebellion brought down increased intensity of pursuit and severe retaliation by the authorities against all Anabaptists.

The Mennonites. The peaceful Anabaptists subsequently became known as "Mennists" or "Mennonites" to identify them with their peaceful leader Menno Simons, and to differentiate them from the "Münsterites" who had participated in the violence.[12] It appears that the name "Mennonites" or "Mennists" did not become widely used in the Netherlands, but came into more general use in Royal Prussia only some time after they fled there from persecution in the Netherlands. In any event, the "peaceful" distinction was not recognized by religious and civic authorities under the emperor Charles V because of his orders to rid his domains of all Anabaptists.[13] Menno himself at that time carried a price upon his head[14] in spite of his counsel for peace, even after converting many of the violent ones to the peaceful cause.

ORIGINAL HOMELAND OF THE
NETHERLANDIC MENNONITES

The netherlandic Low German Mennonites of America are descendants of Anabaptists of the Frisia Triplex who settled in the Vistula-Nogat River delta of the former Royal Prussia prior to their subsequent moves to Russia and to America.[15] Although most of them departed for the Vistula delta from East Friesland, many had not been long-term residents there. They were there because the rulers at that time were tolerantly disposed toward Anabaptists seeking refuge. East Friesland provided a place of assembly and embarkation for refugees who were fleeing the persecution coming from the south and the west.[16] As discussed in a paragraph under "The Peaceful Anabaptists," their numbers were increased by High German Anabaptists from southern Germany and greater numbers of Flemish from Flanders.

Anglo/Frisian/Saxons. To the Frisian/Saxons in the Frisia Triplex, movements of refugees had added south Germans of non-Saxon origin and large numbers of Flemish from Flanders. It should be noted that since Flanders had been settled by Saxons, even before the occupation of Britain, the Flemish were ethnically closely related to them.[20] Consequently, netherlandic Anabaptists of the Frisia Triplex were predominantly of Frisian/Saxon origin. During the occupation of Britain, or even before, the Angles and Saxons had become virtually the same. Many

During the sixteenth century, the Anabaptists in the Frisia Triplex were mostly local Frisians. The Frisian inhabitants of East Friesland[17] and Groningen had by then assimilated so much Saxon influx that they had become virtually indistinguishable from the Saxons.[18] They had also adopted the Lower Saxon language. The people of West Friesland, who remained staunchly Frisian, continued to speak their Frisian language as they still do.

The combined people of the Frisia Triplex were descendants of Frisian and Saxon forebears of whom,one thousand years earlier, many had emigrated to Britain[19] where, together with Angles and Jutes, they had become the English people.

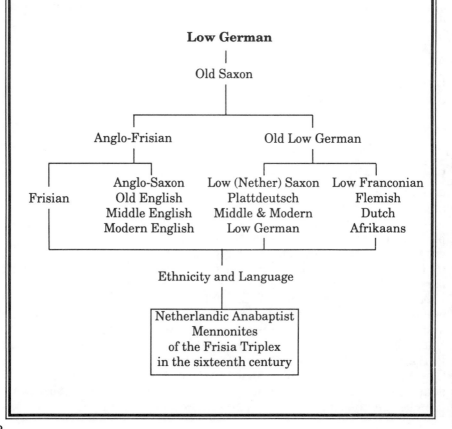

Low German

Old Saxon

Anglo-Frisian   Old Low German

| Frisian | Anglo-Saxon
Old English
Middle English
Modern English | Low (Nether) Saxon
Plattdeutsch
Middle & Modern
Low German | Low Franconian
Flemish
Dutch
Afrikaans |

Ethnicity and Language

Netherlandic Anabaptist
Mennonites
of the Frisia Triplex
in the sixteenth century

Frisians had joined the Anglo-Saxon occupation of Britain at that time.[21] Consequently, the lineage of people who occupied Britain and of those on the Continent from whence they came is seen to have been largely Anglo/Frisian/Saxon. At that time, there was probably little, if any, difference in ethnicity between those who took over occupation of the Island of Britain and those left behind on the European Continent.

Ethnic and language differences existing between people in Britain and those on the Continent at the time of the Reformation and Menno Simons had been brought about by the preceding eleven centuries of eventful and separate histories. The Norman conquest of Britain in the eleventh century was an event with major effects on the English people and their language. The historical separation between the English and those on the Continent in the twentieth century has grown to over fifteen centuries.

LANGUAGE OF THE MENNONITES
OF THE FRISIA TRIPLEX

Nether Saxon Low German. The Anabaptist Mennonites of the Frisia Triplex during the days of Menno Simons mostly spoke Low German, except those in West Friesland. Most of those who fled the Netherlands to settle in the Vistula delta, were native to East Friesland and Groningen, where Nether Saxon Low German was spoken then[22] as it is now. At that time, dialects of Low German spoken to the east of the Dutch Netherlands were termed to be "Oosters" (Eastern). The form of Low German spoken in Groningen and East Friesland, which was also written there by Menno Simons, was termed to be "Oosters gekleurd" (Eastern coloured).[23]

Frisian. The Anabaptists who were native to West Friesland at that time spoke the Frisian language,[24] to which scholars also refer as "Anglo-Frisian."[25] That West Frisian people were not in the majority among Anabaptists who resettled to the Vistula delta is evident in that their descendants today speak a tongue with only a few Frisian words in it. The speech of netherlandic Mennonites is clearly not Frisian,[26] although they are largely of Frisian ethnic extraction.

High German. Those refugees from southern Germany who settled among Anabaptists of the Netherlands, spoke High German or a dialect of it from whence they came. Being in a minority among their fellow Anabaptists, their day-to-day relations with other believers must have accommodated the dominant Low German. Today there are High German names among netherlandic Mennonites among whom some speak only Low German. On the other hand, there is no reason to conclude that High German was ever nonexistent among netherlandic Mennonites. In the Frisian branch of the Mennonite church in Prussia (which the High Germans joined), the ministers preached in High German before those of the Flemish branch.

Flemish/Vlaams. The Anabaptist refugees from Flanders who joined others of their faith in the Frisia Triplex obviously spoke Flemish (Vlaams), which is still spoken in Flanders. It is a Nether Franconian dialect akin to Nether Saxon and readily understood by speakers of it. Consequently, it would not have greatly hampered understanding among refugees in the Frisia Triplex. It eventually yielded uneventfully to the dominant Nether Saxon.

THE WRITTEN LANGUAGE OF THE NETHERLANDIC MENNONITES

Dutch. By the time of Menno Simons in the sixteenth century, the Frisian people in the provinces of Groningen and East Friesland had become Saxonized[27] to such degree that people in both provinces spoke the Nether Saxon language. Although Dutch had already become a written language in the thirteenth century, from which literary Dutch was to emerge,[28] it had been under German, Franconian and Saxon influences to the extent that most people of the Netherlands spoke in various forms and dialects of what they then called Nederduitsch or Dietsch.[29]

The few Anabaptists of the Frisia Triplex who could write at that time probably wrote what one would term to be Dutch. The port city of Emden in the German province of East Friesland was exposed to Dutch influences by tradition and through trade with the Netherlands, therefore much business and record keeping was done in Dutch.[30] Although East Friesland and the city of Emden were German (having been part of the Netherlands for less than ten years during the Napoleonic period),[31] the German language was not officially used in the city until about AD 1700. The upper strata of society in East Friesland changed from Dutch to High German only gradually after 1800.[32]

Those Anabaptist leaders of the Frisia Triplex who wrote, did so in Dutch, as did Menno Simons and as was officially done in the city of Emden. Their correspondence with other Anabaptist leaders in Dutch cities such as Amsterdam, was mostly in Dutch, which those in Amsterdam frequently termed "impure Dutch". A few must have written in Low German (little survives) and some wrote in what we would today call a mixture of Low German, High German and Dutch, which was termed "mengelmoes"[33] (mixture) by Dutch translators. It must not be overlooked that among the early Anabaptists in the Triplex were High German refugees who could and did write in High German, at that time referred to as "Overlandsch."[34]

Frisian/Oosters/Low German. Preserved documents show that Menno Simons wrote a great deal, and that he began writing in West Friesland in the Dutch language.[35] Although he was a native Frisian, his training for the priesthood had equipped him with a mastery of Dutch in a more acceptable form than would be mastered by most other Frisians.[36] Then he moved to Groningen or East Friesland where he continued writing to his flock in "Oosters gekleurd" (Eastern colored), and later in "Oosters" (Eastern).[37] Oosters meant the language to the east of Dutch and Frisian, the Nether Saxon Low German of Germany.[38] During his final years from 1553 until 1561 at Fresenburg in Holstein, Menno wrote and printed his works in the local Low German of Holstein.[39] He also rewrote and republished a number of his earlier writings in the latter dialect[40] which the Dutch termed Oosters. Most or all of his works were translated into Dutch before republication by Dutch Anabaptists (Doopsgezinde) in Holland.

CLARIFICATION OF TERMINOLOGY

Describing language used in Europe in the sixteenth century presents the problem of relating terminology of that time to words as we understand them today. For example, the word "Oosters" was used to describe a language in those days, but means little to us now, because we use other terminology. Further confusing it, the word "Nederduitsch" carries a different meaning to a Dutchman (Hollander) than it does to a German. In addition, the words Niederfränkisch, Dietsch, Holländisch and Niederdeutsch at one time meant more or less the same thing. Consequently, for modern readers to understand sixteenth century terms, the following clarifications provide their meanings in today's terminology:

Old Terminology	Modern English
Duitsch/Dietsch	Netherlandic, including Dutch and Flemish
Nederduitsch[41]	(Dutch)Hollandish or Netherlandic
Niederdeutsch	Low German (Nether Saxon and Lower Franconian)
Oosters/Oostersch[42]	Nether Saxon Low German (East of the Netherlands)
Oosters gekleurd Oostersch gefärbt	Netherlandic with Low German (color) traits
Overlandsch/Oberländisch[43]	(standard) High German

THE OPPRESSOR REACHES INTO THE FRISIA TRIPLEX

West Friesland. The first death by martyrdom of an Anabaptist in West Friesland was recorded in 1531.[44] Then five years later, two Anabaptist followers from Witmarsum were required to appear before authorities to answer charges of harbouring Menno Simons. By then, Menno had left the Roman priesthood and had become elder and leader of the peaceful Anabaptists. This brought down upon him the wrath of the authorities. He was pursued and forced into hiding. It became a capital crime to shelter him. Hermann and Geeryt Jansz were convicted of this crime on the 24th of October 1536 and were both condemned to death.[45]

The fact that the Anabaptist movement had already begun before Menno Simons became one of its leaders (1536) is evident in the first three Proclamations posted against them in Friesland in 1534, in which Melchior Hofmann (erroneously named as Michael Pelser) was named as one of their wanted leaders.[46] By 1536, the Amsterdam Anabaptist church had a membership variously reported between 1,535 and 3,500 persons.[47] From these facts it is clear that Menno Simons was not a founder of the Anabaptist movement. He became one of their leaders at a difficult time after the insurrection at Münster had intensified the hatred of the authorities against them.

Groningen. In 1534, a Proclamation against Anabaptists in Groningen was worded against "alle uitheemische wederdoopers" (all 'alien' rebaptizers).[48] This was apparently intended to get rid of "outside" Anabaptists who had found refuge in Groningen. Another 1534 Proclamation against Anabaptists announced fines and banishment, but still differentiated between "in den Omelandes van Groningen geseten of woenachtig ofte vonbueten inkomich" (established residents of Groningen or outsiders who have come in). A 1535 Proclamation described "Mans ofte vrouwenpersonen in den Ommelanden van Groningen geseten ofte vyn buten inkoemisch" (Men or women in lands around Groningen, established residents or newcomers). A 1539 Proclamation was particularly directed against established residents who had embraced Anabaptism.[49]

East Friesland. During those hard times for the Anabaptists, East Friesland continued to be the more tolerant toward them. A trek of Anabaptist refugees, fleeing for their lives and seeking a haven in East Friesland, began no later than 1528.[50] But, in 1530 the Duke Enno I of East Friesland also issued an edict against them, threatening them on pain of loss of life and limb to leave East Friesland before Shrovetide (preceding Lent).[51] In 1535, adult baptism was banned in East Friesland, which ban was reinforced by a decree in 1537.[52]

Increasingly harsh focus of the emperor Charles V on Anabaptist dissenters in his realm followed in the aftermath of the infamous Anabaptist insurrection of 1534-1535 in the German city of Münster. Intolerance and persecution of Anabaptists thereafter worsened for all Anabaptists because the emperor's retaliation against them did not distinguish between Münsterites and peaceful Mennonites. Since all Anabaptists were religious dissidents, all were subject to consequences of the laws against dissidence.

The Duchess Anna of Oldenburg became ruler of East Friesland after the death of her husband in 1540. She was tolerantly disposed toward peaceful Anabaptists in her domain. However, in 1544 the Holy Roman emperor Charles V[53] directed a proclamation against Anabaptists in which he did not differentiate between peaceful followers of Menno Simons and "sword-minded"[54] (Sweertgeestern)[55] followers of men like Jan van Batenburg and David Joris, who condoned the violent overthrow of established authority. The ominous portent in being equated by the emperor with followers of violence was recognized with apprehension. It showed Menno's peaceful flock how precarious existence in East Friesland had become and convinced many to flee the country.

In the year 1545 there appeared yet another edict, this time directed against the person of Menno Simons himself,[56] apparently after he had already fled to Cologne.[57] Though the Duchess Anna still attempted to differentiate between unruly Anabaptists and peaceful Mennonites,[58] her previous method of avoiding prosecuting them—by issuing strongly-worded edicts, and then not carrying them out—she could no longer employ.[59] In 1549 she was forced to sign an edict "ordering all Anabaptists out of East Friesland." This edict precipitated the departure of her noble adviser á Lasko. These disturbing events emphasized once more how very tenuous any tolerance for Mennonites had become by then.[60]

MENNONITES TREK TO THE VISTULA DELTA

Fortunately, for the Anabaptists during those oppressive times, opportunities for resettlement on extensive land holdings in Royal Prussia opened up to them.[61] This subsequently led to a trek of Anabaptists from the Frisia Triplex to the Vistula River delta and to the city of Danzig, beginning in the 1540's.[62]

Note: More details of the relocation from the Frisia Triplex to Royal Prussia are found under "Sixteenth Century Settlements," Chapter Six.

Records of the city of Danzig show that by 1547 there was a large contingent of Frisian Anabaptists (Mennonites) already living near Danzig,[63] whom Menno Simons visited in 1549.[64] New streams of refugees fleeing from intensified persecution in the Netherlands and elsewhere continued to be recorded for the balance of the sixteenth century[65] and well into the seventeenth.

The great majority of Anabaptist (Mennonite) settlers of the Vistula-Nogat delta and the environs of Danzig came either directly or indirectly from the Frisia Triplex.[66] Some of those from the Netherlands had already been refugees from elsewhere. Among settlers in the Vistula from northeastern Germany during those years, many were already refugees from the Netherlands. For many of the new settlers, this move was only one more in a series of moves in search of a tolerant haven.

Most of the peaceful Anabaptists fleeing to the Vistula delta were of Frisian origin, natives of West Friesland, Groningen and East Friesland. But, among them were refugees from other parts of the Netherlands and Germany.[67]

Their written language. Aside from correspondence between leaders of the Mennonite churches in Prussia and corresponding leaders in the Netherlands (Amsterdam), there is little to indicate which language the Mennonites wrote at that time. The majority of them were or had been citizens of West Friesland, Groningen and East Friesland where Dutch was then the prevailing written language. Consequently, it is reasonable to assume that the writing of most netherlandic Mennonites who could write must have been in Dutch,[68] albeit probably "Oosters gekleurd" (coloured by Low German). It is more probable that most of them, other than their leaders, could not write at all. They are described as simple farmers, occupied with a fight for survival which left little time to think of writing. The Frisians, particularly, were anything but literary minded.[69]

Their spoken language. There can be no doubt that the Anabaptists who settled in the Vistula-Nogat delta generally spoke, and all understood, a loosely-knitted dialect of Nether Saxon Low German. It was and still is the spoken language of the provinces of Groningen and East Friesland. Most of the Anabaptists to settle in the delta of the Vistula had come from Groningen and East Friesland.[70] Their spoken language understandably contained Flemish, Dutch and Frisian influences. By what name they then knew their language, does not seem to be definitively recorded, but in all likelihood it was "Dietsch".

Summary of Chapter Five

When one compares the Anglo-Frisian-Saxon origins of netherlandic Mennonites with the origins of the Anglo-Saxon British, one concludes that the forebears of both were virtually the same people fifteen centuries ago. Mennonite Anabaptists who moved from the Frisia Triplex to West Prussia in the sixteenth century were predominantly of Saxonized Frisian stock who spoke netherlandic Nether Saxon Low German with dialectical variations.[71]

Scholars disagree over the identity of the language in some of Menno's writings. But he came from an area of the Netherlands where most writing was in Dutch, probably mixed with local dialect. Menno's later writings in Groningen or East Friesland were said to be Dutch with Low German colouring. Those among his flock who could write would hardly have done otherwise. "Een jeder deed wat goed was in ziine oogen" (Each did as seemed good in his own eyes).[72] Of course, some of the High German refugees among them would have written in High German.

Anabaptists of peaceful persuasion found East Friesland a temporary haven of refuge because its rulers, especially Anna of Oldenburg, were at first tolerant toward them. She was the first to describe them in her edict of 1545 as "Mennonites" to make the distinction between them and the violent Münsterites. When this tolerance of the Duchess Anna was overruled by the Roman emperor Charles V, who did not make this distinction, the Mennonites were forced to seek asylum elsewhere.

Invitations to them from landowners and city councils in Polish Royal Prussia to settle in the Vistula river valley led to a mass movement of Mennonites and other Anabaptists from the Frisia Triplex to the delta of the Vistula river, beginning about 1540.

NOTES TO CHAPTER FIVE

Note: See Notes to Chapter One for Abbreviations

1. B.H. Unruh, *Die niederländisch-niederdeutschen Hinterqründe derMennonitische Ostwanderungen*, (Karlsruhe: Im Selbstverlag, 1955), p. 8.

2. *Ibid.*, p. 10.

3. *Ibid.*, p. 9.

4. *Ibid.*, pp. 8 & 10, 46-47.

5. *Ibid.*, p. 10.
   —*Encycl. Brit.*, "Frisians", (Chicago: William Benton, Publisher, 1959), Vol. 9, p. 854d.

6. *Ibid.*, "Frisians", Vol. 9, p. 855a.

7. *Ibid.*, "Frisians", Vol. 9, p. 854c.

8. *Encycl. Brit.*, "Reformation", 1959, Vol. 19, p. 39d.

9. Unruh, pp. 23, 36, 46.
   —*Mennonite Encyclopedia*, "Anabaptist", H.S. Bender, (Scottdale: Mennonite Publishing House, 1957), Vol. 1, p. 113.
   —*Encycl. Brit.*, "Anabaptists", 1959, Vol. 1, p. 857d.

10. *Mennon. Encycl.*, "Menno Simons", Cornelius Krahn, Vol.3, pp. 577-583.

11. *Mennon. Encycl.*, "Münster", Cornelius Krahn, Vol. 3, pp. 777-783.

12. Unruh, p. 90.
    —*Mennon. Encycl.*, "East Friesland," Vol. 11, p. 120c.

13. Unruh, pp. 38,39.

14. *Ibid.*, p. 85.
    - *Mennon. Encycl.*, "Menno Simons", Cornelius Krahn, Vol. 3, p. 579.

15. Unruh, pp. 33, 91.

16. *Ibid.*, pp. 35, 36, 88.

17. Karl Bischoff, "Mittelniederdeutsch", *NSL*, p. 108.

18. Unruh, pp. 13,14.

19. *Encycl. Brit.*, "Frisians", 1959, Vol. 9, p. 854b.

20. Unruh, p. 30

21. *Ibid.*, p. 180.

22. *Ibid.*, pp. 8, 13, 14.

23. *Mennon. Encycl.*, "Oosters and Oosters gekleurd," Cornelius Krahn, Vol. 4, p. 70.

24. *Ibid.*, pp. 8, 15.

25. *Ibid.*, p. 13.
    —*Encycl. Brit.* "Frisians," 1959, Vol. 9. p.854b.

26. Jack Thiessen, "The Low German of the Canadian Mennonites", *Mennonite Life,* July 1967, p. 110.

27. Unruh, p. 13.

28. *Ibid.*, p. 16.

29. *Ibid.*, p. 15.

30. *Ibid.*, p. 13.

31. *Ibid.*, p. 7.

32. *Ibid.*, p. 178.

33. *Ibid.*, p. 85.

34. *Ibid.*, p. 79.

35. *Ibid.*, p. 80.

36. *Ibid.*, pp. 32, 33.

37. *Ibid.*, pp. 78, 84.

38. *Ibid.*, p. 77.

39. *Ibid.*, pp. 75, 167.
   —*Mennon. Encycl.*, "Oosters and Oosters gekleurd", Cornelius Krahn, Vol. 4, p. 70.

40. *Mennon. Encycl.*, "Menno Simons", Cornelius Krahn, Vol. 3, p. 583.

41. Unruh, pp. 14,15,16,17,180.

42. Unruh, p. 77, 79.
   —Horst Penner, *Die Ost- und Westpreulßischen Mennoniten*, (Weierhof: Mennonitischer Geschichtsverein, 1978), p. 180. Penner states that Oostersch is the designation for Nether Saxon Low German only in the western part of the Low German language zone. This does not appear to agree with some definitions by others.
   —*Mennon. Encycl.*, "Menno Simons," Cornelius Krahn, Vol. 111, p. 583a.

43. Unruh, p. 79.

44. *Ibid.*, p. 30.

45. *Ibid.*, p. 85.

46. *Ibid.*, p. 23.

47. *Ibid.*, p. 24.
   —*Mennon. Encycl.*, "Amsterdam", Fr. Kuiper, Vol. 1, p. 101b.

48. Unruh, p. 31.
   —*Mennon. Encycl.*, "Groningen", N. van der Zijpp, Vol. 2, p. 589b.

49. Unruh, p. 39.

50. *Ibid.*, p. 36.

51. *Ibid.*, p. 37.
   —*Mennon. Encycl.*, "East Friesland", Cornelius Krahn, Vol. 2, pp. 119-122.

52. Unruh, p. 37.

53. *Encycl. Brit.*, "Charles V.", Roman Emperor and (as Charles l) King of Spain, Vol. 5, p. 260c.

54. *Mennon. Encycl.*, "Batenburg, Jan van," J. Loosjes, Vol. 1, p. 247b.

55. Unruh, p. 40.

56. *Ibid.*, p. 89.

57. Horst Penner, *Die Ost- und Westpreulßischen Mennoniten*, (Weierhof: Mennonitscher Geschichtsverein e.V., 1978), p. 33.

58. Unruh, p. 90. The first recorded instance of the use of the name "Mennonites" (Mennisten) to distinguish the peaceful Anabaptists followers of Menno Simons from the followers of David Joris and Battenburg came in an edict unwillingly issued in 1545 by the Duchess Anna of Oldenburg, ruler of East Friesland.
   —*Mennon. Encycl.*, "East Friesland," Cornelius Krahn, Vol. 11, p. 120.

59. Unruh, p. 89.

60. *Ibid.*, p. 39.

61. *Ibid.*, p. 89.
  —*Encycl. Brit.*, "Albert," (1490-1568),1959, Vol.1, p. 522b.
  —*Mennon.Encycl.*, "Albrecht," Christian Hege, Vol. 1, p. 35a.

62. Unruh, p. 32.

63. *Ibid.*, pp. 39, 91.

64. *Mennon. Encycl.*, "Menno Simons," Cornelius Krahn, Vol.3, p. 581.
  —*Mennon. Encycl.*, Danzig refugees," Walter Gering, Vol.2, p. 12.

65. Unruh, pp. 31, 32,135.

66. *Ibid.*, pp. 33-36.

67. *Ibid.*, p. 46.

68. Jack Thiessen, "Mennoniten Plautdietsch. Woher? Wohin?" *Der Bote, 1. April 1992,*
  Nr.14, p. 4.

69. Unruh, pp. 32,33.

70. *Ibid.*, pp. 181-182
  —Horst Penner, p. 180.
  —Tjeerd de Graaf, "In Siberië' spreken ze Grunnings," (Groningen: *Trojka Magazine.*
  March 1992. After his 1991 visit to Mennonites living in Neudachino, near Omsk in
  Siberia, Dr. de Graaf, a Professor at the University of Groningen reports (in a trade
  magazine): "Mennonites in Siberia speak the (Nether Saxon) dialect of Groningen."

71. Jack Thiessen, "Mennoniten Plautdietsch, Woher? Wohin?", *Der Bote. 1. April 1992,*
  Nr.14, p. 4.

72. Unruh, p. 80.

CHAPTER SIX

The Language of the Mennonites in Prussia

Teutonic Prussia

The original Baltic inhabitants of the territory along the southern shores of the Baltic Sea, later to become known as Prussia, were the "Old Prussians" (Pruzzen, Prusi or Borussi).[1] Early in the thirteenth century, the land they inhabited was Polish territory. In 1226 the Polish Duke Conrad of Mazovia invited the Teutonic Order of Knights to enter this territory to combat the native Prussians whom he had been unable to subdue.

The Knights of the Order came and conquered the Prussian territory. Through a difficult struggle they exterminated or drove out most of the Old Prussians. After these successes, the Knights consolidated their position and extended their influence northward along the Baltic coast as far as Esthonia. These conquests in the Baltic by the Knights of the Teutonic Order had the blessings of the pope and the emperor.

As the name Teutonic implies, the knightly Order was German. Therefore, the Knights invited German peasants and townspeople to occupy and settle their conquered territories. With the help of these settlers, they built towns and castles from Danzig Bay up the Vistula and Nogat river valleys as far southward as the present cities of Kulm (Chelmno) and Thorn (Torun').[2]

At that time, German merchants of the Hanseatic League established and carried on trade in the Baltic and Vistula river port cities of Danzig, Elbing, Marienburg, Thorn, Königsberg and others. In the development of trade and commerce in the Baltic region before 1350, merchants of the League led the way.[3] Since the Hanseatic League consisted of a consortium of north German cities whose language of business was Low German, their business activities and their building of settlements introduced and fostered use of the Low German language in all cities in which they traded.

The administrative language of the Order of Knights was Middle High

63

German. Merchants of the Hanseatic League, on the other hand, spoke Low German as did many of the settlers brought in by them and by the Knights. Consequently, a major segment of the population below senior administrative levels spoke Low German. The overall character of the Prussian state became and remained German,[4] albeit a mix of High German and Low German.

In the fifteenth century, Germanization of the populace and military strength and ambitions of the Teutonic Prussian state had grown to proportions that threatened Poland. Military conflict became inevitable. The ensuing battle was a victory for Poland, being aided by the cities of Danzig, Elbing and Thorn. The Peace of Thorn in 1466 forced the defeated Knights to cede all of West Prussia to Poland under the name of Royal Prussia.[5] The eastern portion became known as East or Ducal Prussia whose Teutonic Duke would henceforth be subservient to Poland.

After 1466, the previously-Germanized Prussia again came under the domination of Poland. West Prussia under the name of Royal Prussia, was ruled directly by the Polish king who extended special priveleges to such cities as Danzig, Elbing and Thorn in reward for their aid in battles against the Teutonic Order. East Prussia under the name of Ducal Prussia remained self-governing, but its Grand Master was forced to be a vassal of the Polish king.

SIXTEENTH CENTURY
SETTLEMENTS

Lowlands of Royal Prussia. The lowlands of the Vistula river delta lay centred in the triangle formed by the cities of Danzig, Elbing and Marienburg, and reached southward up the Vistula-Nogat river valley and eastward toward and beyond Lake Drausen (Map #5, p. 66). For agricultural development, these bottom lands presented problems similar to those in areas of the Netherlands. The flood plain of the delta was barely above sea level, some of it even below. In the 1540's, vast expanses of it were virtually unproductive swamps, lying under annual flooding of the Vistula river, and overgrown with swamp grasses, reeds and willows.[6]

Although dikes had been built and drainage ditches had been dug by earlier settlers of the thirteenth century, those early improvements had fallen into disrepair due to wars and neglect. The limited agricultural development achieved at that time, had been wiped out by subsequent flooding. Yet, these early attempts at farming had indicated that the lands were indeed fertile.

At about the time of the religious persecutions of the Anabaptists in the Netherlands, the Duke Albrecht of Brandenburg, the councils of the cities of Danzig, Elbing and Graudenz, as well as independent landowners formulated policies to encourage suitable farmers to relocate to the Vistula/Nogat delta and river valley to redevelop and expand agricultural production on large tracts of their unproductive, water-logged lands.[7] The most logical place to find people with the necessary expertise and ability to dike and to drain the delta lowlands was in the Netherlands.

The landowners of Royal Prussia were well aware of this, and they also knew that religious persecution and its threat in the Netherlands was causing numbers of Dutch Anabaptist farmers there to look afield for places to resettle.[8] Consequently, appropriate steps were taken by those city councils and landowners to invite people from the Netherlands to resettle in the Vistula/Nogat delta.

Anabaptists in the Vistula delta. When the invitation to resettle in the lowlands of the Vistula river was received by the Anabaptists in the Frisia Triplex, it seemed an answer to prayer. The needs and the desire to escape were great. Here was the opportunity. It opened the door to resettlement in a land of relative peace, such as could be found nowhere in the Empire of Charles V. (Roman Emperor and King of Spain).[9] Before long, the decisive move to the Vistula delta gained momentum.

When, in about 1540, the Anabaptist migrants began arriving in what might have been aptly named their new "Prussian Netherlands," they settled into an area where the landscape and the language of the people were much the same as those from whence they had just departed. Their agricultural experience in the Netherlands had taught them how to drain low-lying lands and how to build dikes to prevent flooding. They were thus ideally prepared to bring the Vistula delta into agricultural productivity, and they went to work and did it.[10] This story of their language shall not dwell on the vicissitudes encountered by those Anabaptist farmers in the delta, nor of their agricultural successes. But, the results of several decades of their activities and successes would have justified the name "Prussian Netherlands" for the Vistula delta. The Anabaptists and their descendants became noted for their industry, for their farming production and for their transformation of the delta from swamplands to agricultural masterpieces. (Note: The peaceful Anabaptist followers of Menno Simons were first officially referred to as Mennonites [Mennisten] in East Friesland by the Duchess Anna in her edict of 1545. But, they did not become generally known by that name until somewhat later in Royal Prussia)

Languages of the Vistula Delta. When the new settlers began arriving in the delta of the Vistula and Nogat rivers in the mid-1500's, many areas were already partially inhabited. Previous colonization by German peoples brought in by the Teutonic Order and the Hanseatic League[11] had given the region a German character.

Although the Teutonic Knights and the language of their Order[12] were mostly Middle High German, the colonists who followed them to occupy the conquered lands were predominantly Low German, peasants from various parts of northern Germany.[13] Their Low German origins are evident in many old place-names in Prussia, most of which (for subsequent political reasons) have been changed.

As early as AD 1240, citizens of the city of Elbing obtained a "Rechtskodex" (Code of Legal Rights) which was written in Low German.[14] So entrenched was Low German in Prussia and even farther

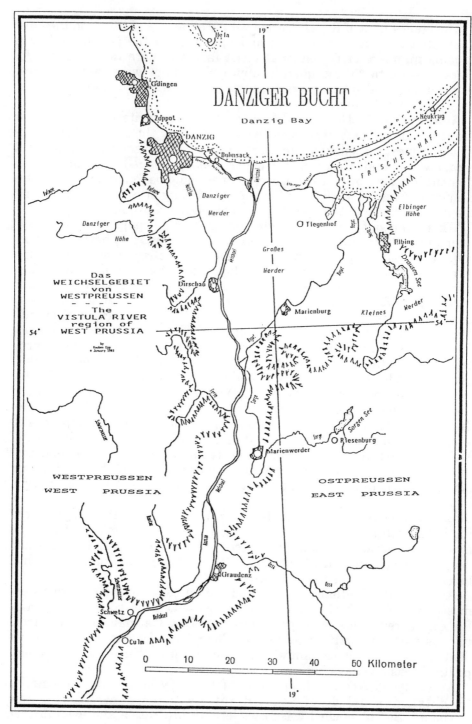

DANZIGER BUCHT

Danzig Bay

Das
WEICHSELGEBIET
von
WESTPREUSSEN
- - - -
The
VISTULA RIVER
region of
WEST PRUSSIA

WESTPREUSSEN

WEST   PRUSSIA

OSTPREUSSEN

EAST   PRUSSIA

0   10   20   30   40   50 Kilometer

Map #5

north along the coast as a result of colonization by the Teutonic Order and the Hansa, that in the city of Riga, Latvia, the Reformation took place entirely in Low German.[15]

Spoken Language of the Vistula delta. At the time of the first Mennonite settlements in the delta of the Vistula river and the city of Danzig shortly after 1540, Royal Prussia had already been under Polish rule since 1466. Preferential treatment of the city of Danzig and its environs had left its High and Low German character largely intact. Local inhabitants spoke a dialect of Nether Saxon Low German[16] that was understandable to the incoming Netherlanders. The new settlers adopted the "Ostniederdeutsch" (Eastern Low German) manner of speech of their new Prussian neighbors,[17] but also imparted to it a number of words and characteristics from their Western Low German of the netherlands.[18] One scholar states that the Nether Saxon dialect was "spoken exactly the same" in Groningen as it was in Danzig.[19] Although one questions "exactly the same" in such widely separated localities, "great similarity" is nevertheless indicated. With relatively minor adjustment to their own dialect, Mennonites in the delta continued speaking much as they had in their former homeland.

These forebears of the netherlandic Mennonites of the Americas, whose language is a subject of this story, lived for more than two centuries (1540-1789) in Royal Prussia (which later became West Prussia) after settling there from the Frisia Triplex. Although some of them also settled in other parts of Prussia on first arrival or subsequently, the great majority stayed in the Vistula delta until large numbers of them moved to New Russia. Low German, as spoken among Mennonites in America who came here via Russia, is still oriented to the manner in which it was spoken in the Vistula delta at the time of their leaving there.

It is well to note that the language of the delta at that time was in a state of flux (shift),[20] which meant that people in a given area at one time in its history spoke the dialect differently from the way it was spoken there at another time. There were also pronounced differences in speech among people in one region, such as between social levels or between rural and urban people or between the rich and the poor.

If, as scholars have indicated, there was at that time an ongoing pronunciational shift in the spoken language, responsible for differences in the way it was spoken by those of the 1788-89 settlement in New Russia and those of the later 1804-06 movement,[21] then such differences would become the more apparent among those whose forebears remained in Prussia at that time, but who resettled in Germany and America more than a century later.

Spoken Dialects of West
and East Prussia. [22]

An examination of the Low German of Prussia is complex because there were nine different dialects of Nether Prussian spoken in the two parts of Prussia,[23] in addition to two of High Prussian and one of Schwäbisch. Since East and West Prussia together represent a land area only about one half the size of the state of Florida or one tenth of the province of Manitoba, it is apparent that moving from one locality to another brought the Mennonites into contact with a number of dialects in addition to those that they had brought with them from Groningen, East Friesland and Flanders.

This exposure to a multiplicity of dialects at least partly explains why there are now so many variations in manner of speech among them. And it is also the reason why there are at least two other distinct dialects of Prussian Low German among Mennonites, in addition to the dominant Plautdietsch.

Plautdietsch. The dialect of Low German spoken by the great majority of Mennonites in West Prussia was that of the Werders (Danziger Werder, Großes Werder and Kleines Werder)[24] at the heart of the Vistula delta. Since the Mennonites were not literary minded, there is little written record of how it was spoken by them at that time. Voice recordings were, of course, unknown.

One of the distinctive characteristics of their speech was that they usually pronounced the "a" in closed syllables as "au".[25] Plautdietsch is still spoken this way. In English, the difference would be similar to pronouncing "hall" as "howl".

Another characteristic of Plautdietsch was/is the peculiar tendency to palatalize pronunciation of the consonant "k"[26] in certain contexts. This pronunciational peculiarity is described as emanating from East Pomeranian (hüttenpommersch) influence.[27]

As an example, the Plautdietsch verb infinitive "to look" is spoken "kjikje(n)" (some speak the "n", others don't). In Low German in general this verb is spoken as "kieken, kicken or keken" without palatalization of the "k". In English, similar palatalization of the "k" consonant (in this case spelled "c") is found in the word "cute", which may be compared with "coot" to hear the difference that palatalization makes.

Some speakers of Plautdietsch shift the palatalized "k" forward in the mouth to form a palatalized "t", in which case the verb infinitive "to look" is actually spoken as "tjitje" or "tjitjen". It is not unlike the pronunciation of the English word "church" which is a palatalized way of pronouncing "kirk".[28] (More on Plautdietsch pronunciations in a following Chapter).

Karolswalde (Kulmerland) Dialect. As noted, Mennonite settlers in Prussia were exposed to a number of dialects. A sizable group of them that had settled in the vicinity of Culm (Map #5, p. 66) were located among speakers of the Culmerland (Kulmerland) dialect.[29] A contingent from this settlement subsequently resettled into Volhynia at about the time of another major resettlement from the Danzig area to the Chortitza Colony of the Ukraine. Among the Mennonite villages established in Volhynia was Karolswalde,[30] which name has stayed with them in America in describing their origin and dialect. In Karolswalde and their

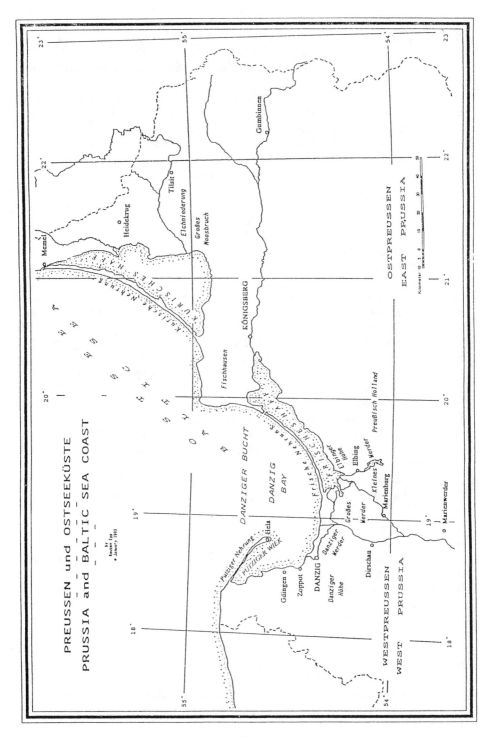

Map #6

other villages, these Mennonites lived in relatively closed communities, out of daily contact with speakers of other dialects of Low German. Therefore, their Kulmerland dialect did not change much under outside language influences while there.

They subsequently resettled directly from Volhynia to Kansas and South Dakota in the 1870's without undergoing the "melting-pot" process of living in large Mennonite settlements which shaped the Plautdietsch of major groups in the Ukraine. One still notices in the speech of the Karolswalde group and their descendants the distinctiveness of the Kulmerland.[31] Although their dialect is readily understood by most Low German Mennonites, one would not call it Plautdietsch. Those of the Karolswalde dialect (as in most dialects of Low German), pronounce "a" where speakers of Plautdietsch pronounce "au". (In English, it is as the difference between "ha" and "how"). This is only one difference among others. Consequently, the Karolswalde speaker does not speak of his dialect as "Plautdietsch"; he calls it "Plattdietsch".

Dialect of the Eastern District, (Mundart des Ostgebietes).The Eastern District dialect, one of the nine major dialects of Prussia, was spoken in the region to the east of Kurisches Haff, in the general area of the city of Tilsit, including the Elchniederung (Map #6, p. 69). In about 1713, the area was in part resettled by about fifty families of Mennonites from Royal Prussia on invitation of Frederick I of Prussia to take up agriculture in those areas depleted of resident farmers by a plague from 1709 until 1711, which had killed off fully 40% of the population.[32] When the Mennonites settled there, they inevitably adopted the manner of speech of their East Prussian neighbors and continued to speak it there until 1945. From the district of Gumbinnen, East Prussia, thirty families joined the 1788 Mennonite movement to the first (Old) colony in Russia (then known as New Russia).[33]

A written record of this dialect is contained in a book[34] in which Trude Janz relates numerous short stories in the Nether Prussian dialect of the Eastern District. This dialect also does not follow the distinctive "au" for "a" pronunciations so characteristic of Plautdietsch from the Vistula delta.

High German in Royal Prussia. The Teutonic Order of Knights, founders of the Germanized Prussian state, spoke and wrote Middle High German. Polish rulers after 1466 do not appear to have had much influence over language in Royal and Ducal Prussia, nor were there major incursions of the Polish language into German where it was already established.

Administration of the city of Danzig was so thoroughly Low German that official communications from that city to other governments continued in Low German until about 1560. The last Low German letter from Danzig city hall was sent in 1563.[35] After that, High German was used in all official communications of the city, despite the continuing sovereignty of Poland.

Although official matters were dealt with in High German in Royal Prussia during the latter part of the sixteenth century, the people below senior administrative levels and those on the land remained relatively unaffected by High German. The Mennonites continued to speak their Low German among themselves, using it or Dutch as their language of worship. Although some of them obviously mastered High German earlier, their churches did not generally change to its use in worship until the end of the eighteenth century.

In nineteenth century West Prussia, Mennonite young people learned in their schools about the "fineness" of High German[36] as compared to their everyday Low German. Such teaching left its impression upon them. However, the vigour of their Low German language did not remain subdued by High German after leaving school, except among the young ladies. The ladies preserved their acquired "finer" High German even after they were married, using it exclusively in conversations with their Low-German-speaking husbands and maids. The young men, on the other hand, returned to their accustomed use of Low German, as they had done in the homes of their elders. Only after the 1870's, was there a gradual shift toward greater use of High German in Mennonite homes in Prussia.

WRITTEN LANGUAGE IN PRUSSIA

When the Mennonites arrived in Royal (Polish) Prussia in the sixteenth century, those among them who could write, ministers and community leaders, usually wrote in Dutch. The leaders in the Frisian churches led the way toward writing in High German in the seventeenth century. They were also the first to use High German in worship services in the eighteenth century. In Flemish churches, particularly in the city of Danzig, they kept the Dutch language in worship and in church record-keeping much longer. Only after 1780 did they yield to the use of High German. The probability that most Mennonites in Prussia did not write much seems to be borne out by the lack of surviving writings from the several centuries of their sojourn there.

FRISIAN AND FLEMISH MENNONITES

Early settlements of Mennonites in Royal Prussia usually built a local church to serve the community. Such a congregation would be a member of either the Frisian or Flemish wing of the Mennonite church. A dispute over matters of doctrine had begun between the two ethnic groups while they were still in the Netherlands. When their differences could not be resolved by them at that time, it resulted in a division into Frisian and Flemish branches of the Mennonite church.

When they moved to Prussia, this division was carried with them. But, in the course of time, membership in either branch came to be determined more by matters of faith than by ethnicity. Frisian families whose names appeared on the register of a Frisian church, might subsequently

71

appear on the register of a Flemish church, or vice versa. This story of the Low German language shall not delve into theological differences among Mennonites then nor now. Suffice it to say that such disputes among Mennonites of Frisian ancestry are reminders of the character traits of Frisian people who, early in their history, were known for their habit of feuding with each other.

The Frisian Church. The High German language entered the Frisian/Flemish equation when the High German refugees among them joined themselves to the Frisian branch of the church. This contributed to an earlier switch to High German among the Frisians, as was evident in their High German letters written in 1671 by leaders of the Frisian churches in Royal Prussia to their sister churches in Amsterdam.[37] Obviously, Frisian church leaders would not have written to Amsterdam in High German if they had also mastered Dutch. Although some worship services among the Frisians may have been conducted in Low German in the eighteenth century, church records among them were kept in High German after about 1723.[38] High German was accepted as the language of worship among the Frisians of the Werder before it was accepted in the city churches of Danzig.

The Flemish Church. In the Flemish branch of the church, unlike the Frisians, recordkeeping in the Danzig church continued in the Dutch language for several generations longer. So "Dutch" was the Flemish church in West Prussia, that exchanges of ministers in both directions took place between them and Amsterdam well into the 18th century.[39] Dutch was the language of the pulpit in Danzig until 1780; only after that did it yield to High German.[40]

Summary of Chapter Six

The Anabaptists settled into the Vistula river delta of Royal Prussia in the sixteenth century from the Frisia Triplex of the netherlands, where the majority of them spoke the Nether Saxon Low German of Groningen and East Friesland. Upon arrival in Prussia they found that the resident population also spoke Low German which they could easily understand. The netherlandic Anabaptists adopted the dialect of their neighbors, but imparted to it numerous netherlandic words and expressions brought with them.

During their first years in Royal Prussia they were known simply as Dutch Anabaptists. These peaceful Anabaptists later came to be known as Mennonites to distinguish them from other Anabaptists of less peaceful persuasion.

The language of the common people of Prussia at that time was largely Low German; top officials spoke the Middle High German of the Teutonic Order, even in those parts of Prussia directly under Polish rule. The Teutonic Knights had brought in Low German settlers and others to occupy lands conquered from the original Prussians. By the middle of the sixteenth century, while the people still spoke Low German, city administrations and government and judicial offices were gradually changing to High German in their correspondence.

The last Low German letter left Danzig city hall in 1563.[41] Thereafter, official matters came to be dealt with increasingly more in High German, while the ordinary people continued speaking Low German among themselves as before.

Whereas Prussian cities, officials and administrative systems had by this time largely changed to High German, the netherlandic Mennonites (except those who were already High German) did not convert from Low German or Dutch to High German as their language of worship or correspondence until more than two centuries later, and even then not uniformly nor totally.

When the Mennonites left for New Russia in their migrations of 1788-89 and in the early years of the next century, the Dutch language had almost ceased to be used by them. The Low German Plautdietsch dialect, with variations, was spoken by all. Few Mennonites at that time could write. Of those who could, most wrote in High German,[42] but some still wrote in Dutch.

NOTES TO CHAPTER SIX

Note: See Notes to Chapter One for Abbreviations

1. *Encycl. Brit.*, "Prussia," 1959, Vol.18, p.652d
   —*A Homeland for Strangers,* Peter J. Klassen, (Fresno, California: Center for Mennonite Brethren Studies, 1989), p. 5.

2. *Ibid.*, p. 5.

3. *Encycl. Brit.*, "Hanseatic League", 1959, Vol. 18, p. 162c.

4. *Encycl. Brit.,* "Prussia," 1959, Vol.18, p. 654b.
   —Unruh, p. 173.

5. *A Homeland for Strangers,* Peter J. Klassen, p.6.
   Encycl. Brit., "Prussia," 1959, Vol.18, p. 653a.

6. Jack Thiessen, "Variations in Mennonite Plautdietsch", *Mennonite Quarterly Review*, 1988, p. 286.

7. B.H. Unruh, *Die niederländisch-niederdeutschen Hintergründe,* (Karlsruhe: Im Selbstverlag, 1955), p. 89.

8. *Ibid.*, p. 89.

9. Horst Penner, *Die Ost- und Westpreußischen Mennoniten,* (Weierhof: Mennonitischer Geschichtsverein, 1978), p. 33.

10. Although, as has been said, these Mennonite farmers were not 'literary-minded', they were certainly agricultural pragmatists, as their successes demonstrate.

11. *Encycl. Brit.*, "Hanseatic League," 1959, Vol.11, p. 162b.

12. Artur Gabrielsson, "Die Verdrängung der mnd. durch die nhd. Schriftsprache", *NSL*, p. 145.

13. Karl Bischoff. "Mittelniederdeutsch", *NSL*, pp. 99-100.
    —Jack Thiessen, "Low German (Plautdietsch) in Manitoba," (University of Winnipeg, 1986) p. 130.

14. Walther Ziesemer, *Die Ostpreußischen Mundarten,* (Wiesbaden: Dr. Martin Sändig oHG., 1979), pp. 101-103.

15. Artur Gabrielsson, "Die Verdrängung der mnd. durch die nhd. Schriftsprache," *NSL*, p. 146.

16. Penner, p. 180.

—Dieter Stellmacher, *Niederdeutsche Sprache*, Langs Germanistische Lehrbuchsammlung, Band 26, (Bern: Verlag Peter Lang AG, 1990), p. 137.

17. Unruh, pp. 123-124.

18. Erhard Riemann, *Preußisches Wörterbuch*, (Neumunster: Karl Wachholtz Verlag, 1974), Einführung, Bd. 1, Lfg. 1, p. 6.

19. Penner, p. 180.

20. Jack Thiessen, "Low German (Plautdietsch) in Manitoba," (University of Winnipeg, 1986) p. 186.

21. Jack Thiessen, "Mennoniten Plautdietsch, Woher? Wohin?" *Der Bote. 1. April 1992*, Nr.14, p.4.

22. For the purpose of discussing the languages of Prussia, this writing shall consider West Prussia to be that which at one time was Polish or Royal Prussia, including the city of Danzig (now Gdansk) and its territory (See Map #5, p.66). East Prussia is considered to be that part of Prussia lying to the East of West Prussia, including former territories as far to the north as the city of Memel, past the northern tip of Kurisches Haff (See Map #6, p. 69).

23. Ziesemer, Map p. 137.

24. Jack Thiessen, "Variations in Mennonite Plautdietsch," *Mennonite Quarterly Review*, 1988, p. 288.

25. Jack Thiessen, "Low German (Plautdietsch) in Manitoba," University of Winnipeg, 1986, p. 132.
—Ziesemer, p. 132.

26. Jack Thiessen, "Variations in Mennonite Plautdietsch," *Mennonite Quarterly Review*, 1988, p. 293.

27. Ulrich Tolksdorf, "Die Mundarten Danzigs und seines Umlandes," *Danzig in acht Jahrhunderten*, (Munster: Nicolaus-Copernicus-Verlag, 1985), p. 322.

28. Jack Thiessen, "Variations in Mennonite Plautdietch," *MQR*, July, 1988, p. 286.

29. Ziesemer, p. 137.
—Erhard Riemann, *Preußisches Wörterbuch*, 1974, Bd. 1, Lfg. 1, p. 3.

30. *Mennon. Encycl.*, "Karolswalde," (Scottdale: Mennonite Publishing House, 1957), Vol.3, p. 152.

31. Ulrich Tolksdorf, Leiter: Preußisches Wörterbuch, Neue Universität, Haus N 50c, Olshausenstraße 40/60, D-2300 Kiel, Germany. In response to a cassette recording of an interview with speakers of the Karolswalde dialect in Nebraska in 1987, and forwarded by this writer to Dr. Tolksdorf, he replied: "Es ist einfach erstaunlich, wie sich die Mundart des Kulmerlandes über 200 Jahre so deutlich erhalten hat."
Note: This writer has been notified that Dr. Ulrich Tolksdorf died on the 9th of September 1992 at the age of 54 years.

32. Ulrich Tolksdorf, *Eine Ostpreußische Volkserzählerin*, (Marburg: N.G. Elwert Verlag, 1980), p. 38.

33. Horst Gerlach, "Von Westpreußen nach Rußland," *Westpreußen Jahrbuch. Bd. 41*, (Münster: Westpreußen Verlag, 1991), p. 104.

34. Ulrich Tolksdorf, *Eine Ostpreußische Volkserzählerin*, (Marburg: N.G. Elwert Verlag, 1980).

35. Artur Gabrielsson, "Die Verdrängung der mnd. durch die mhd. Schriftsprache," *NSL*, p. 145.

36. Walter Quiring, *Die Mundart von Chortitza*, quoting Regehr's of 1902, in Q's note #66, p. 47.

37. Penner, p. 178.

38. *Ibid.* p. 179.

39. *Ibid.*, p. 181.

40. Unruh, p. 175.

41. Gabrielsson, "Die Verdrängung der mnd. durch die nhd. Schriftsprache," *NSL*, pp. 145-146.

42. Walter Quiring, *Die Mundart von Chortitza in Sud-Rußland*, (Druckerei Studentenhaus Munchen, Universität, 1928), p. 47.

CHAPTER SEVEN

Language of the Mennonites in Russia and America

Resettlement from West Prussia to New Russia

When the Mennonites migrated to New[1] Russia after a sojourn of almost two and one half centuries in Polish Royal Prussia, their use of Dutch in worship had been practically discontinued,[2] although it was still read by a few.[3] High German had only begun to take its place in worship and in writing.[4] In official Prussian circles, the High German legacy of the Teutonic Order remained a strong influence even under Polish sovereignty after 1466. The chanceries (offices of administration) of all cities except Danzig had changed to use of High German by 1500. The city of Danzig made the change somewhat later; the last official Low German letter was sent out by the administrative offices of that city in 1563.[5]

Despite being surrounded by High German at city "official" levels, few Mennonites of the early migrant waves to Russia of 1788-89 and the first decades of the 1800's, had more than a rudimentary knowledge of it.[6] Day-to-day conversation was almost totally in the Low German dialect (or dialects) to which they had become accustomed in the Vistula delta.

Low German was so widely used among them that it was also the language of instruction in many Mennonite schools in Russia during the first several decades there.[7] The Russian and High German languages were both considered by Mennonite children to be foreign.[8] In conservative congregations church services continued to be held in Low German, as is done by some in Canada and Mexico to this day.

Mennonites were not German Colonists. Since the Mennonites enjoyed a measure of local self-government[9] within an administrative apparatus of the Russian state,[10] village life and affairs were conducted in Low German. At that time they did not regard themselves as "German" colonists, even though they had come to Russia from Hohenzollern Prussia. Nor were they perceived by others to be either German or Prussian.[11] They had little affinity for High German, and held

75

Russian and Ukrainian in low esteem. Few Mennonites attained competence in Russian during the first several decades in Russia. The government had a policy to carry out official correspondence with Danzig Lutheran colonists, Swedish colonists and the Mennonites in High German. According to Rempel[12] this was done to preclude frequent excuses of colonists that they misunderstood Russian Law and directives. The policy of administering Mennonites in High German presented a problem because they were especially unskilled in bureaucratic High German.

The Mennonites in Russia made improvements to their system of education as early as the 1820's, but major changes came about in general reforms of their school system and its governance in the 1840's under influences of Johann Cornies. The language of instruction thereafter became High German.[13] Even then, no concerted move was made toward teaching Russian. Only a few individual teachers ventured to do so.

The Great Reforms of Russian society, which began in 1861, included in 1870 the setting aside of special rights of all colonists, including Mennonites.[14] In the 1870's, the government cancelled the remaining autonomy that Mennonites enjoyed in operating their schools under the Ministry of State Domains, and in 1881 placed them under administration of the Russian Ministry of Education.[15] Teaching of the Russian language would thereafter become compulsory.

Since prospects for economic prosperity were becoming increasingly better, Mennonites were at first not concerned when compulsory attendance at school was reduced both in years and in hours per week. However, the continuing threat of repressive measures by a hostile Russian Ministry of Education awakened many of them to greater interest in education and in the system that the Ministry sought to restrict. This stimulated greater sacrifices to preserve their schools. One result was that increasing numbers of young Mennonites attended teacher training institutions and universities in Russia and Western Europe, especially in Germany.[16]

The wholesome consequence of developing better-qualified teachers was that Mennonite youth thereafter enjoyed the benefits of more competent instruction in the German and Russian languages. This opened up to them the riches of literature in both.

Dialectical Differences in Low German in Russia

Some assume that the Old Chortitza and New Molotschna Colony characterisitics of Low German speech originally developed in those colonies because of their isolation from each other.[17] But, scholars have shown that speech characteristics existing in the various localities from whence they came in Prussia were brought with them into Russia, where they became the characteristics upon which the spoken language in each colony developed.[18]

Since the Mennonites who settled in Russia came from various parts of the Vistula/Nogat delta and river valleys, and from the vicinities of Danzig, Marienburg and Elbing, as well as from Brandenburg, Volhynia and East Prussia, these scattered places of origin determined that although they all spoke the same language there were distinctive speech differences among them. Quiring quotes Regehr[19] who explains that in each of the four major Mennonite settlements: Danziger Nehrung, Danziger Werder, Große Marienburger Werder and Kleine Werder, the spoken dialect often differed more from that of neighboring districts than from the more distant dialects of East Prussia. There were nine dialects of Nether Prussian spoken in East and West Prussia.[20] Consequently, when groups of Mennonite families from scattered areas gathered at points of assembly for the move to Russia, the larger group of migrants spoke a mixture of dialects.

When a contingent of migrants who speak different dialects of the same language establishes a colony together, some homogenization of dialect is bound to take place. Such was the case when the Chortitza Colony began in 1789. Thereafter, wave after wave of additional settlers brought added diversity of speech to the colony. In two decades after the first settlement, the colony had reached a population[21] in the order of 2,000 to 3,000 persons.

When, in 1804, about 75 miles distant, settlement of the Molotschna Colony began, additional waves of settlers, and in greater numbers over a longer period of time, brought its population in four decades to about 14,000 to 15,000 persons. Settlers of this "new" colony were of greater diversity in their places of origin and manner of speech than were those of the earlier colony. This colony embodied a different dialectical mix.

These colonies became melting pots in which Plautdietsch developed characteristics peculiar to each colony. Speech of the dominant segment of inhabitants of a colony would tend to prevail,[22] but there continued to be in-colony variations.

THE OLD COLONY: CHORTITZA

When Mennonites first began their migration from West Prussia to New Russia in 1788-89, the Prussian government refused exit permits to landowners and wealthy families.[23] Consequently, those with land or wealth could not legally leave at that time. Only the landless and the poor were permitted to realize their desires to get out of Prussia and to avail themselves of opportunities offered by the Russian government. For that reason, first contingents of Mennonites to resettle in Russia were mostly from the poorer working class of Danzig[24] and the Danziger Nehrung. The majority of them were from the Flemish branch of the church.[25] But, before long, others joined them, including thirty families from East Prussia.[26]

Old Colony Speech Characteristics. The foregoing factors in large measure determined the mixture of dialects the first group of migrants brought with them to Russia. Those characteristics of their mother tongue dominated the manner of speech in the first colony from its beginnings. The influence of other characteristics of speech brought in by later groups of settlers probably shaped speech in the colony, but did not become dominant. The manner of speech that thus became typical of the first colony in Russia was later termed to be Old Colony Plautdietsch. A few of its differences from speech as heard in the later Molotschna (New) Colony are listed as follows:

a. The "u" in words such as "Du" (you) [singular], "Ju" (you) [plural], and "Hus" (house) is usually modified by Old Colony speakers to "Dü," "Jü" and "Hüs."[27] To those who speak only English, suffice it to say that a German "u" as in these examples (without the umlaut) is pronounced as in "flute". The German "ü" is difficult for the speaker of English to pronounce because it is not heard in English. In this context it consists of "oo" (as in soon) and "ee" (as in seen), but spoken together.

b. Verb infinitives usually end with "en",[28] as opposed to New Colony verbs in which the "n" is dropped. Examples are "backen" (to bake) and "gohnen" (to go/walk), which in the Molotschna subdialect are spoken as "backe" and "gohne."

c. Verbs in the first, second and third person, plural forms usually end with "en" as in wi/ji/se "doonen," "sinjen" and "spälen." This is common to eastern Low German and that of the Netherlands. In the Molotschna colony the final "n" of these verbs is dropped in this context, and they are spoken as wi/ji/se "doone," "sinje" and "späle." Dropping a final "n" in this context is characteristic of most Prussian dialects.

d. Nouns, which in the Molotschna subdialect end with a schwa, as in "Retze" (cracks), "Däare" (doors) and "Kroage" (collar), are spoken in the Old Colony as "Retzen," "Däaren" and "Kroagen" or "Kröagen."[29]

e. The vowel "o" of the "oa" diphthong, as in "moaken" and "vondoag" is often modified by umlaut to "ö" as in "möaken" and "vondöag."[30] For speakers of English only, correct pronunciation of this modified diphthong is at first well nigh impossible.

f. Palatalization of "k" is common in both Old and New Colony Low German, as shall be discussed later in this chapter.[31]

g. The Westgermanic syllable "aw" appears in Old Colony Low German as "eiw" in such words as "bleiw" (blue), "greiw" (grey), "Meiw" (sleeve) and "heiwen" (to mow),[32] as opposed to "blau," "grau", "Mau" and "haue" in some other dialects. The subdialect of the Molotschna eventually came to harmonize with the latter.

The New Colony: Molotschna

When the Mennonites first began leaving West Prussia for Russia in 1788, many more would have left, but the Prussian government did not permit owners of land or wealth to emigrate. However, within fifteen years, the ban on emigration had been modified to a ten percent exit tax.[33] By then, emigration to a second colony in Russia was underway and many more families had prepared to make the move. Smith says that first settlers of the 1803-06 migration were from among wealthier Mennonites,[34] and in greater numbers from the districts of Elbing and Marienburg.[35]

Since first settlers to the Old (Chortitza) Colony were largely of the poorer working class of people from Danzig and Danziger Nehrung, whereas those to the New (Molotschna) Colony were wealthier Mennonites from the districts of Elbing and Marienburg, such differences in status and places of origin determined that they also had dialectical differences in their manners of speech.

Some scholars logically point out that migrations of Mennonites to the Chortitza (Old) Colony and to the Molotschna (New) Colony took place during a time period when a language shift was taking place in Prussia.[36] Language shift may change the characteristics of speech in a given area over a comparatively short period of time. Scholars have established that traits of speech among settlers who moved to Russia no longer existed in their original Prussian settings several generations later.

One wonders whether a language shift in Prussia during the time of the first and second Mennonite migrations to Russia contributed more to their speech variations than did speech differences related to their differences in status and locations in Prussia. One must agree that a language shift in Prussia could have had a marked bearing on speech differences between waves of settlers to Russia. But, those differences were imposed upon variations already existing, and as determined by their social and economic status and places of abode. People coming from the areas of Danzig, Marienburg and Elbing would have represented a number of many dialectical variations among Nether Prussian dialects.

In any event, the dialectical mix among first settlers to the New Colony was different from that of the earlier Old Colony. Combined, these factors shaped the spoken Low German that grew and became characteristic of the Old (Chortitza) Colony and of the New (Molotschna) Colony.

The 1772 Partition of Poland renamed Royal Prussia as West Prussia and placed it under Hohenzollern Prussian jurisdiction. Hohenzollern policy stressed the use and teaching of High German in schools.[37] In several decades, this policy exerted its influence on the language of Mennonites in West Prussia, as became evident among settlers in later migrations to Russia.

New Colony Speech Characteristics. Following are some speech variations characteristic of the Molotschna subdialect:

a. The "u" in words such as "Du," "Ju" and "Hus" are also frequently partially modified as in "Dü, Jü and Hüs," but noticeably less so than in the Old Colony. Some Molotschna families pronounce the "u" completely unmodified, resembling the English "oo" in soon and coot, or the German "u" in Busen and Hut.

b. The "en" endings of verb infinitives, common to Chortitza speakers, are dropped in favour of "e" (schwa) endings as in other Prussian dialects.

Therefore, Molotschna speakers would say, "Wi woare fesche gohne" (we shall go fishing), whereas Old Colony speakers would say, "Wi woaren feschen gohnen."

c. Verbs in the first, second and third person plural forms, which in most eastern Low German dialects end with "en", drop the "n" and retain a schwa as in wi/ji/se "backe" and "gohne."

d. Nouns, which in the Old Colony subdialect end with "en" as in "Retzen" (cracks), "Däaren" (doors) and "Kroagen" (collar) are spoken in the Molotschna subdialect as "Retze," "Däare" and "Kroage," in which the final "e" is spoken as a schwa.

e. Palatalization of "k" is also common in the Molotschna Colony. This palatalization will be further discussed under "kj" and "tj" Pronunciational Differences.

f. The Westgermanic syllable "aw" is usually considered common to the Molotschna manner of speech. It was certainly looked upon by Molotschna colonists as the "correct" manner of speech after their first century in Russia, but there is increasing evidence to indicate that it was not always so. This aspect of pronunciational change will be further discussed under Molotschna Dialect before and after 1870. The first post-World-War-I immigrants came to America in the 1920's with the "aw" syllable firmly entrenched in the Molotschna subdialect in words such as "blau" (blue), "grau" (grey), "Mau" (sleeve) and "haue" (to mow).[38]

THE VOLGA MENNONITE SETTLEMENTS

Beginning in 1853 some five hundred families from West Prussia and eighty families from Galicia[39] resettled into Russia after all available farmland in the Chortitza and Molotschna colonies had been taken up. The Russian government allocated them land along the Volga river.[40] The Volga Mennonite settlements were located in the province of Samara, in a district known as the "Trakt." The first settlement Köppenthal was followed by a second which began in 1861, known as Old Samara. These settlements later formed part of the Volga (German) Autonomous Republic. The entire German-speaking population of that republic was exiled to Siberia in 1941.

Volga Speech Characteristics. Mennonites in the Volga colonies spoke a Low German dialect somewhat different from the Plautdietsch of the Old colony or the Molotschna Colony . In the poem "Die Heimfahrt nach Preußen" (The journey home to Prussia), Johannes Harder[41] includes fragments of Volga Plautdietsch which indicate that the "a" in a word such as "dat" (that) was not spoken as "au" in "daut," as would be done in the Chortitza or Molotschna colonies. The "k" in "eck" is not palatalized and the "u" in "Hus" is not umlauted. The following Low German portion from the poem illustrates those differences: "Jungs senn ji doa? Met nejentich Joa, woat endlich Tied, dat no Hus eck foa" (Boys, are you there? At ninety years, it's finally time that I drive home).

80

Differences in the Volga Low German may stem partly from the fact that they left West Prussia almost half a century later than the Molotschna colonists did. Scholars acknowledge that the fifteen years separating the Chortitza and Molotschna settlements (1789-1804) created language differences between the two colonies because of a language shift taking place at that time in West Prussia. Another fifty years under the Hohenzollerns preceding the Volga settlements could well have created the added differences.

Political changes in West Prussia determined an ongoing change in spoken and written languages there at that time. In 1772, Polish Royal Prussia passed to Hohenzollern Prussian jurisdiction as West Prussia. The subsequent movements of West Prussian Mennonites to Russia began after less than two decades of direct Prussian rule over them. By the time of the settlements along the Volga river, the settlers from West Prussia had been under Prussian rule for eighty years. Those additional decades of Hohenzollern High German influences left their marks upon their language.

Another factor contributing to differences in the language of the Volga settlers was that a contingent of some eighty families from Galicia (according to Unruh) joined the five hundred families from West Prussia to form the first Volga settlement group. The Galician Mennonite families were largely of Swiss and south German origin,[42] certainly not Low German. They added to the infusion of High German in the speech of the Volga settlements. This tends to explain why Harder would use the following sentence in his poem: "Was wirden die in Preißen sonst sagen— wann eck ankoam as so'n ruscha Pracha" (What would those in Prussia say—if I should arrive there like some Russian beggar). The first half of the sentence is in High German as spoken by Mennonites of the Volga settlement.

The Volga Mennonites did not resettle to America in large numbers as did those from the Chortitza and Molotschna colonies. Therefore, their manners of speech did not become a major component of the Plautdietsch of Mennonites in America.

OTHER MENNONITE COLONIES
IN RUSSIA

The two major Mennonite colonies in New Russia (later to become the Ukraine) and their dialectical differences have been discussed here. Since their manners of speech largely determined how Low German is spoken among Mennonites today, this story shall not dwell on other smaller colonies beyond mentioning some of them.

Volhynia. At about the time of the founding of the Chortitza Mennonite colony, there was a relatively small migration from the area of Graudenz near Culm. After some initial difficulties, this group settled in the vicinity of Ostrog in Volhynia,[43] east of the city of Kiev. They spoke the Culmerland dialect, which they later called the Karolswalde dialect after one of their first villages near Ostrog. The Karloswalde colonists resettled in the states of Kansas and South Dakota in 1874.

Daughter Colonies. As the populations of the Mennonite colonies grew, the supply of colony land for young people ran out. This problem was solved by establishing daughter colonies, beginning with Bergthal Colony by the Old Colony in 1836, to be followed by numerous others created by both major colonies, mostly after 1860.[44] Although daughter colonies were frequently at some distance from mother colonies, these colonists continued to speak the subdialect of their mother colony with whom they stayed in close and frequent contact. In daughter colonies jointly founded by the Old Colony and the New, such as near Orenburg, some homogenization of dialect began to take place.

The 1870's — Crossroads in Russia

The pivotal 1870's formed the central decade in an era of progress and reform in education that was to become decisive in the future and language of Mennonites in Russia.

In the nineteenth century, Low German so dominated the speech of Mennonites that in the first decades in Russia it was frequently used as language of instruction in their schools and of worship in their churches. They began to take steps toward teaching High German in the 1820's, advances that continued through generations after the 1870's. Earlier progress in education, enabled by bringing in instructors of German from among German Lutheran colonists and Mennonites in Prussia, was confirmed and expanded by educational reforms under Johann Cornies in the 1840's.

Focus on language instruction was further sharpened by the Great Reforms brought in by the Russian government in the decades between 1861 to 1881. Although Mennonites had initiated the teaching of Russian in some of their schools by about 1830, the new reforms required that the language become a compulsory subject in all colonist schools. These prospects prompted Mennonites toward more emphasis on German to preserve their non-Russian identity.

The spiritual awakening which led to a separated Mennonite Brethren denomination in the 1860's was introduced by evangelists from Germany[45] who preached in High German. German religious books contributed to this movement and helped to acquaint them with the language. Low German[46] was at that time still much used in worship and in preaching among them, as is evident in their concern over its "appropriateness" for this purpose.

RUSSIAN GOVERNMENT REFORMS OF 1861-1881

Two major policies of the reforms instituted by the Russian government in the period between 1861 and 1881[47] formed the crossroads at which Mennonites in Russia chose the direction that would affect most aspects of their future, lives and language. Those general reform policies, directed toward all colonists in Russia, applied to the Mennonite perspective as follows:

a. The Mennonite school system would be deprived of the measure of autonomy it had enjoyed until then under the Ministry of State Domains, and would thereafter be placed under a hostile Ministry of Education. Teaching a number of subjects in the Russian language would become compulsory.

b. All Mennonite men would henceforth be conscripted into the armed forces for a period of non-combatant service. (This requirement was later modified to conscription into a civilian organization performing forestry service, controlled and financed by Mennonites, but under state juridiction.)

A Russian Eternity. The consternation created by these policy announcements among Mennonites in Russia at that time can be appreciated when viewed from their understanding that their request for military exemption had been freely granted and confirmed before they first settled in Russia.[48] Although the subject of language in their schools does not appear to have been specifically addressed by the "Privilegium" (Charter of Rights and Privileges), awarded to the Mennonites by Imperial Decree (Ukase) of the Czar on the 8th of September, 1800,[49] their promised exemption from military service in perpetuity certainly was, as it was to all foreign colonists.

Management of their own school affairs, and the language of instruction, was regarded by them as one of their religious freedoms and rights. Religious freedom had been guaranteed by the Czar's Charter, but that charter specified neither language nor school affairs. They, however, felt that freedom of choice in language was necessary for them to maintain their separate identity and "religious Apartheid,"[50] which was not Russian. The prospect of compulsory use of Russian in their schools and threats of further Russification, meant to them loss of their identity.

If they had misperceived their rights in matters of schools and language, no such misperception was possible in understanding their exemption from military service for all time.[51]

Their "Privilegium" was regarded by Mennonites as a "sacred trust" bestowed upon them by the mighty Czar of Russia. Many saw the actions of the Russian government of 1870 as a violation of that "trust." This created widespread alarm. Especially among more conservative elements, most of them resolved that such violation of trust could not, and would not, be accepted. Therefore, they would leave Russia as a matter of conscience. The Russian eternity had indeed ended!

Choice of Directions. This prompted a search for an alternate country in which to resettle. With this in view, Canada and the United States received immediate and foremost attention. The Mennonite attitude toward placating reassurances by the Russian government was now jaundiced by the fact that what had been promised to them for all time had lasted less than a century.

83

Split Decision. When the Russian government became aware of the Mennonite reaction, it delegated Adjutant-General Totleben to forestall any possible mass exodus by seeking a compromise with the Mennonites. Totleben promised a form of service that would be non-military, and emphasized excellent prospects for economic well-being (which in fact proved to be true). In little more than a week, two thirds of the Mennonites in Russia at that time were persuaded to stay.[52] The other third, joined by all of the Hutterites, consisting of the Old Colony Bergthal and Fürstenland assemblies, some Chortitza groups, the Molotschna Kleine Gemeinde and Alexanderwohl congregations, and many others, moved to Canada and to the United States between 1874 and 1880.

Low German Mennonites in America

Several major movements of Mennonites from Russia to the Americas have taken place; one in the nineteenth century and two in the twentieth. The initial reasons for these movements were dissatisfaction with changes in Russian government policies that threatened to force them to compromise their principles. In the twentieth century, dissatisfaction took on more basic dimensions.

MIGRATION TO AMERICA IN THE 1870'S

The first major movement of Mennonites from Russia took place in the 1870's. At the time, it first appeared that most of them would leave because of their dissatisfaction with changes in Russian government policies toward them. Part of the dissatisfaction was tied to the language question in that the government threatened to impose Russian language instruction in all Mennonite schools, and indicated further moves toward forced Russification of all colonists, including Mennonites.[53] The single major cause for dissatisfaction was the Russian government's cancellation of the exemption from military service, which had been guaranteed in perpetuity.[54] When the government became concerned over the possibility of a large-scale exodus of Mennonites, who were major contributors to the economy, they placated the concerns of the majority by modifying their policies. But, before 1880 about 15,000 to 18,000 (one third of the Mennonite population of Russia) left for Canada and the United States.[55]

The Molotschna migrants (except Kleine Gemeinde) settled in Minnesota, Nebraska and Kansas. Therefore, the Plautdietsch spoken in those States was largely that of the Molotschna Colony of the 1870's. Large contingents from the Bergthal and Fürstenland settlements of the Old Colony settled in Manitoba,[56] where they were joined by the Kleine Gemeinde group from the Molotschna. Consequently, both major subdialects from Russia were well represented in separate settlements in Manitoba.[57]

Note: In the late 1800's Canada opened its doors to homesteading on its central prairies. As a result, at the turn of the century, many first generation Mennonites from the United States and Manitoba took up homesteads in what was later to become Saskatchewan. These resettlements brought to the central prairies Low German manners of speech from both major colonies in Russia. In their somewhat separated settlements at that time, the variations of the Chortitza and Molotschna Colonies were well represented.

MIGRATION TO AMERICA OF THE 1920'S

During World War I and the ensuing period of unrest and lawlessness at the time of the revolution in Russia, large numbers of Mennonites died of illnesses such as typhus; others were massacred by marauding bandits and their goods were plundered. People and their communities were disrupted, pillaged and ravaged. After suffering war, revolution, anarchy and famine, another migration movement of Mennonites to America sought to escape the ongoing disintegration of their way of life and the threat of communism.

The migration of the 1920's totalled about 25,000,[58] of whom 21,000 came to Canada. The remainder went to Mexico and South America.[59]

It became apparent to Mennonites in Canada that immigrants coming from Russia in the 1920's had a more progressive attitude toward education than was common among those already in Canada. Their school system in Russia during the previous fifty years had indeed given them impressive advantages. The newcomers stood out in their mastery of the German and Russian languages. Such superiority was much admired by most, but jealously despised by those who didn't have it. This contributed to tensions between "Russlända" (those recently from Russia) and "Kanaudja" (the established Canadians). Seventy years later (in the 1990's), the terminology is still used but with diminished acerbity.

MIGRATION AFTER WORLD WAR II

After the end of World War II in 1945, another 12,000 Mennonite refugees eventually found their way to Canada and to South America. They were the successful third of many more thousands who made their way out of the Soviet Union with the retreating German army to seek refuge in Germany at the end of the war. From among this large contingent of refugees, 23,000 fell victim to the terms of the Yalta agreement before securing their hoped-for refuge in the West. They were gathered and turned over to Soviet occupation forces who sent them by boxcar into the silences of Siberia and into central Asia.[60]

High German among Netherlandic Mennonites

When the netherlandic Mennonites first began resettling from Prussia into Russia, most of them had only a rudimentary knowledge of Standard (High) German. Although German Anabaptists of south German origin had joined the netherlandic Anabaptists during their escape from religious persecutions of the sixteenth century, they were in a minority and had mostly joined the Frisian branch of the church. This factor contributed to earlier change among the Frisian churches in Prussia to the use of German in worship.

The low level of competence in High German among Mennonites during their first half century in Russia is borne out in the fact that few families among settlers in America in the 1870's spoke High German, yet all spoke Low German fluently. Naturally, among them were those who could speak, read and write German, although perhaps not in a very scholarly manner. After all, their German-speaking ministers were drawn from their own ranks, as were their school teachers.

MENNONITES BECOME GERMAN

The first moves by Mennonites in Russia toward greater use of German came in the 1820's and through the 1840's. Particularly this latter period, was influenced by Johann Cornies. Management of their school system was overhauled. High German gradually came to replace Low German wherever it was still used in instruction. However, qualified instruction was frequently lacking.[61]

The Great Reforms of 1861-1881 intended to promote use of the Russian language by making it compulsory for all colonists to teach it in their schools. This prompted the Mennonites also to engage qualified school teachers to teach a number of subjects in High German.[62] These changes toward High German confirmed and reinforced their earlier school reforms leading up to the 1840's. In effect, it confirmed acceptance of High German as "their" written language.

However, these developments did not bring about a sweeping change toward use of spoken High German. Their Low German continued to be strong and vigorous throughout their sojourn in Russia. It received substantial reinforcement in its use in the forestry camps established by Mennonites in agreement with the Russian government. In the camps, their young men served three-year periods of assigned noncombatant service as alternate to service in the armed forces.

Forestry camps became islands of Low German where use of High German or Russian (except by visiting ministers and camp officials)[63] was discouraged and mercilessly ridiculed by the young men (Forsteier) of the forestry corps.[64] This reinjected vigour into the use of Low German among Mennonite young men and helped to diminish dialectical variances between colonies and villages.

Paradoxically, Mennonites had gradually come to embrace the German language about three centuries after first settling in Royal Prussia, and more than half a century after leaving there and resettling in Russia.

QUALITY OF MENNONITE HIGH GERMAN

As is inevitable when a people nurtures a language in isolation from its mainstream (Germany), pronunciations and expressions characteristic of Mennonites in Russia set their spoken German[65] apart from the language as spoken in Germany. Moelleken describes the High German of the Mennonites as a radical departure from standard German. He labels it "Mennonitisches Standard-deutsch" (Mennonite Standard German), and thereafter refers to it as MSD[66] at its best and as "Dummy High"[67] at its most disfunctional.

Idiosyncracies in spoken German. Since most of the variant tendencies in spoken German of Mennonites relate to their first language Low German, they form an inherent part of this story about Low German. A few of the more noticeable idiosyncracies heard are here listed:

a. The "r" is rolled off the tip of the tongue (in the northern German manner) of the Mennonite speaker in both Low and High German. The uvular "r" is foreign to those not trained in Germany.

b. The German prefix "ge" or initial "g" in such words as "geduldig" and "Gnade" are usually pronounced "je" or "j" as in "jeduldig" and "Jnade."

c. There is little or no differentiation in the quality of "a" in words such as "mahnen" and "Mann" or "Rahmen" and "rammen."

d. The long "o" in "groß," "Boot" and "Moos" takes on Low German overtones (becomes a diphthong) and is pronounced "gro^{u}ß," "Boo^{u}t" and "Moo^{u}s."

e. The long "e" in "See" and "Tee" becomes a diphthong as in Low German, and is pronounced "See^i" and "Tee^i."

f. There is a tendency to use Low German words or expressions in High German, or to make translations that are neither complete nor correct. A few examples are:

   1. The Low German word "drock" is frequently used in place of "beschäftigt," which means "busy."
   2. The word "Hock" is used in place of "Verschlag," which means "pen," as in pigpen.
   3. The word "Großkinder" is frequently used in place of the more generally accepted "Enkelkinder," meaning "grandchildren."
   4 "Ein paar Jahre zurück" is a word-for-word translation of Low German "een poa Joah trigj," which means "a few years ago." In German it could be more acceptably worded, "vor einigen Jahren."

g. There is frequent failure in pronunciation to distinguish between "ie" and "ü" in words such as "vier" and "für" or between "i" and "ü" in "missen" and "müssen."

h. "Bäume" may be pronounced as "Baime" or "Beime" and "heute" may become "haite" or "heite."

i. To these pronunciational and wording peculiarities are added the grammatical problems that confront speakers of Low German who are accustomed to considerable laxity in accusative and dative cases and to a simple wording change in the genitive. When faced with speaking or writing in German, in which the cases are meticulously observed and methodically indicated, Low German speakers are usually in difficulty.

The foregoing are only a few of the more noticeable oddities common to spoken (High) German among Mennonites in America.[68] By contrast, however, those among them who have received schooling in Germany are noticeable in their avoidance of such idiosyncracies.

Plautdietsch: Language or Dialect?

Those who think of Mennonite Low German (Plautdietsch) as a language of its own rather than as a dialect of Low German will surely agree that the question of language or dialect must be based upon conclusions of scholastic research.[69]

This story of Low German presupposes that readers accept language and dialect distinctions published by qualified scholars who have researched Low German and Plautdietsch. Although Mennonite study centres in America are not noted for emphasis on studies in Low German, a number of universities in Europe (as detailed in Chapter Eight) are much involved in its study, including the Mennonite dialect of it. It is from publications by those universities and their professional people, as well as by other language professionals, that the following conclusions are taken and submitted.

The consensus of their findings is that Mennonite Low German (Plautdietsch) is a "Mundart" (dialect)[70] of the Low German language.[71] More particularly, it is one of the Lower Saxon dialects of Eastern European Low German. It falls within the Nether Prussian classification of eastern Low German dialects because of its Prussian origin and dialectical content, as do all Low German dialects of Prussia. Scholars classify Prussian Low German as "Niederpreußisch, Niedersächsisch-Niederpreußisch" (Nether Prussian, Nether Saxon/Nether Prussian).[72] Thiessen describes the Plautdietsch of the Mennonites as a Lower Saxon vernacular.[73]

It is a dialect laced with Netherlandic, German and Slavic loan words, borrowed and absorbed into the mother tongue of its speakers during their sojourns along the way from the Netherlands to Russia. This process continues in whatever country Plautdietsch is spoken today. Sadly, the homeland of Plautdietsch no longer exists, nor is this Mennonite mother tongue heard[74] where once it flourished.

SUBDIALECTICAL VARIATIONS IN
PLAUTDIETSCH

Most speakers of Mennonite Low German are well aware of the differences in Plautdietsch as spoken in the Chortitza (Old) Colony and the Molotschna (New) Colony in Russia. Those differences extend to their respective daughter colonies and to their settlements in America. Several scholars have studied those differences and have written research papers about them.

Loan Words. As is the case in any language, speakers of Plautdietsch have a good vocabulary of words to convey accustomed and everyday concepts. But, in moving from Prussia to Russia to America they were confronted with new concepts for which they did not have suitable vocabulary. In such cases they often used the foreign term, which then became familiar and was accepted. One example is the Russian/Turkish word "backlezhan" for "tomato," first encountered in Russia. It was accepted as "Bockelzhonn" or "Bockelzhaun" and has been used by them for "tomato" ever since. Until then, Mennonites had been unfamiliar with tomatoes and therefore had no name for them. Word adoptions from other languages took place among speakers of Plautdietsch in all countries in which they settled.

Such borrowed "foreign" words together with pre-existing speech variations in their language have led to inconsistencies in the quality or "purity" of Plautdietsch among Mennonites.

Earliest Language Study — Quiring 1928. The first published scholarly study by a Mennonite on the Plautdietsch dialect as spoken in Russia was a Dissertation by Walter (Jacob) Quiring in 1928.[75] Unfortunately, much information about the dialect and its variations from the time of the first settlements in Russia was not available then, nor is it available now. It would have been particularly valuable to obtain information for the period before the 1870's, when little of it was recorded in writing and voice recordings did not exist. A few studies have been undertaken since then, each dealing with Chortitza or Molotschna subdialects or both, in Russia or America. None seem to place particular emphasis on time periods, nor do they relate speech variations to developmental periods or eras in Plautdietsch as it evolved and was spoken in Russia or elsewhere.

Time Periods and Language Change. In the study of a dialect and its development, time periods must be considered together with geographical locations or environmental conditions because time is a variable that brings change to a language. It is not possible, for example, for a language study conducted among Mennonites in Russia in 1928 to have accurately revealed how Plautdietsch was spoken there before 1870. In the absence of earlier research information, 1928 was half a century too late. Educational advances in the intervening fifty years in Russia brought many changes to the speech of Mennonites.

After the Great Russian Reforms of 1861-1881, Russian and German languages were increasingly taught in Mennonite schools. This language training, coupled with increased exposure to spoken Ukrainian, inevitably influenced their spoken dialect. Of course, after a number of generations, Plautdietsch would have undergone normal evolutionary change in any event.

Social Environment and Language Change. A survey, whose results might have been fairly representative of the pre-1870 Molotschna dialect, could have been undertaken among migrants from Russia during their first decades of settlement in Minnesota, Nebraska and Kansas. At that time, the migrants in the States were isolated from changes taking place in Russia, and consequently tended to retain their pre-1870 manner of speech for a longer period. In America, modifying influences were probably less intense and certainly unconnected to exposure to the Russian and Ukrainian languages. However, such a survey was not undertaken. Consequently, we cannot be sure which of the earlier 1800's characteristics of speech might have been recorded three quarters of a century later. Language does not remain static; what is not recorded in its time and in its place is lost forever.

Mennonites of Canada and the United States were not exposed to Slavic languages at work and in school, or to increased use of German in their schools. Once in America, the Mennonites and their speech were exposed to the influences of their new English-speaking neighbours. Their community isolationism on the sparsely inhabited steppes of Russia was not possible in America. A century later, Mennonites in Canada and the States do not realize how much English they have adopted into their everyday Low German, but visitors from other countries do. In the end, the country in which people live determines even how they speak their own mother tongue.

Two Centuries of Plautdietsch

Some of those who are interested in the Plautdietsch dialect, and the changes that have taken place in it, do not seem to realize how such differences and changes were affected by passage of time, by political changes and by differences in geographic locations. Some ascribe the dialectical variations in Plautdietsch to either of the two major colonies in Russia (Old Chortitza or New Molotschna) without reference to events, the passage of time, or movement between continents, all of which also brought about speech differences.

MOLOTSCHNA DIALECT BEFORE AND AFTER 1870

Among the earlier migrants of the 1870's from the Molotschna Colony to Minnesota, Nebraska and Kansas, it was usual to pronounce (to mow) as "heiwe," (blue) as "bleiw" and (to chew) as "keiwe." When the later Molotschna "Russlända" of the 1920's came to America, the established settlers of the 1870's heard that it was more "refined" and less Old Colonyish to pronounce these words as "haue," "blau" and "kaue." Some began to emulate this supposed "refinement." But, that did not explain why pronunciations such as "heiwe," "bleiw" and "keiwe" sounded Old Colonyish or less refined. Few of the migrants of the 1870's to the United States ever spoke with "en" verb and noun endings or other pronunciations typical of the Old Colony manner of speech, and therefore they did not consider their speech to be Old Colonyish.

Some understanding of this conundrum regarding "refinement" may be provided by David Rempel when he says: "The feeling of smugness and self-satisfaction was much stronger among the Molotchnaya Mennonites than among the Chortitza people."[76] Such "smugness" among Molotschna people and, as Henry Dyck states, "an implicit feeling (even in the cultural centres of the Chortitza Colony) that the Chortitza dialect was coarse and `ungebildet' (unrefined)," was coupled with "a general tendency to achieve a refinement suggested by High German."[77] Consequently, when the Molotschna people became more familiar with High German as a result of more intensive teaching of it in their schools, they began to modify their Low German manner of speech in imitation of the "refinement" of High German. Molotschna Mennonites in Russia who until then had spoken "heiwe," "bleiw" and "keiwe" were persuaded by their newly-acquired appreciation for "refinement" to change to "haue," "blau" and "kaue," which more closely resembled High German. Some came to regard Low German as "prost" (uncouth) and discontinued using it altogether in favour of High German. Others attempted to dress it more "correctly" by applying the grammar of High German to it, where it neither fits nor belongs.

The degree of "High German refinement" in the speech of these major colonies was somewhat related to colony levels of smugness and self-satisfaction. As aforementioned by Rempel, those attitudes were stronger in the Molotschna Colony than they were in the Old (Chortitza) Colony.

Those already in America missed such "refinement" in Russia by leaving before the impact of increased German language education had taken its effect. Being largely unaware of subsequent language changes in Russia, they continued speaking their accustomed Low German and to say "heiwe," "bleiw" and "keiwe."

The "kj" and "tj" pronunciational difference. Would-be writers of Mennonite Plautdietsch wrestle inconclusively with how to write the palatalized "k" because some speakers consciously pronounce a "k" whereas others make it a "t." Words like "Kjoakj or Tjoatj" (church), "Kjäakj or Tjäatj" (kitchen) and "Kjinja or Tjinja" (children) are examples of two spoken forms and two controversial ways of spelling the same words.

Solution of the orthographical aspect of this difference shall not be attempted here, but the origin of "kj" and "tj" is of significance to the story of the language (dialect). Firstly, Thiessen and Tolksdorf confirm that the original palatalized consonant is a "k,"[78] which is proven by reading Low German. Both scholars attribute palatalization of it to influences from East Pomeranian (Kaschubian) dialects with whom Mennonites came into contact. They also confirm that East Pomeranian dialects embody the palatalized spoken form as either a "k" or a "t." Such palatalization, which Thiessen describes as a fairly recent development, is not prevalent in all dialects of Prussian Low German, nor in Low German generally.

One concludes that the Mennonites affected by this influence in Prussia, which Tolksdorf terms "hüttenpommersch," were sufficient in number to at least partially entrench palatalization in the speech in both colonies in Russia. In harmony with the East Pomeranian influences, some pronounced the palatalized "k" as "kj" and others as "tj." Since Low German was at that time largely unwritten, there was nothing in writing to decisively indicate whether they were speaking a palatalized "k" or "t." In any event, the inconsistency did not affect communication.

Some ascribe the "kj" enunciation to one major colony (either Chortitza or Molotschna) and the "tj" to the other. However, such ascription is not consistently corroborated when manners of speech of different generations from both colonies are examined.

The "kj" form of palatalized "k" is more consistent among those of the 1870's migration, whether from the Old Colony or the New. In other words, Mennonites in Canada or the United States whose forefathers immigrated in the 1870's more consistently articulate: "Kjoakj," "Kjäakj" and "Kjinja." Furthermore, when asked to spell the word they usually begin it with a "k."

Speakers of the 1920's migration, on the other hand, quite consistently say, "Tjoatj," "Tjäatj" and "Tjinja," and insist that they are pronouncing a "t." A probable cause for this is that Mennonites in Russia after 1870 spoke the Russian and Ukrainian languages more than had previous generations. The increased use of both languages by Mennonites came about because Russian had become a compulsory school subject and Mennonites were increasingly coming into more daily contact with their Ukrainian neighbors, whom they hired as workers and household servants.

The Russian language embodies a palatalized "t"[79] similar or almost identical to the palatalized "k" in Plautdietsch. Speakers of Plautdietsch in Russia knew their palatalized "k" only from the hearing of it, and inconsistently as aforementioned. Therefore, one can understand how students becoming familiar with the Russian palatalized "t" would recognize it as similar or identical to the palatalized "k" in Plautdietsch. Consequently, it would become a logical "next step" to emulate the consistent Russian "tj" when articulating the inconsistent "kj" or "tj" in Plautdietsch. Whether or not one can prove at this late date that the palatalized "t" in Russian reinforced the "tj" pronunciation of the palatalized "k" in Plautdietsch, there remains little doubt that "tj" is more common than "kj" among speakers who also speak Russian.

Vocabulary Changes. The half century between migrations of the 1870's and the 1920's also brought about other changes in manner of speech in Russia which were obvious to Mennonites in Canada when immigrants began arriving in the 1920's. Although the two groups understood each other well enough, there was occasional need to clarify certain words which the new immigrants brought with them. Use of such words contributed to setting the "Russlända" (immigrants from Russia) apart from the "Kanaudja" (Canadians).

Vocabulary Differences. A few of the more noticeable vocabulary differences that the new arrivals brought with them are as follows:

1. A staple of Mennonite diet anywhere is meat balls or rounded meat patties. Since living in Prussia more than two hundred years ago, meat balls were known to them as "Klopps," as they still are among descendants of the 1870's migration. The name is appropriate because the Low German verb "kloppe(n)" means to "beat" or to "pat." When the 1920's immigrants arrived from Russia, they called meat balls "Kotlette(n)," which is not Low German and was unknown to those in America. "Koteletten" is German for cutlets or chops, but a misnomer for meat balls or patties.

2. In Plautdietsch, a noun of masculine gender is changed to feminine by adding the suffix "sche." The addition of "sche" in Plautdietsch is equivalent to adding "ess" in English as in changing the masculine noun "host" to the feminine "hostess." The Plautdietsch word for teacher is "Leahra." When 1870's migrants to America first became acquainted with female teachers (they had had few or none in Russia before then), they followed simple and customary logic to convert the masculine "Leahra" to apply to a female schoolteacher by calling her a "Leahrasche." However, the 1920's immigrants to Canada did not use the word "Leahrasche," they were by then using "Lehrerin," which is High German for a female teacher. Perhaps, this sounds more "refined," but Plautdietsch it is not. The feminine suffix "in" does not belong in Plautdietsch.

3. The word for overcoat was traditionally "Äwarock." The newly-arrived Russlända called one either "Paleto" (which seems to stem from Russian and/or French) or "Mauntel," which (with the "au") is the Plautdietsch way of saying "Mantel" (cloak) in German.

4. The traditional Mennonite word for garlic was "Knoffluach" or "Knoofluach," still common in the United States. The immigrants brought with them the name "Tschisnik" (from the Ukrainian word "Tschisnuk"), which thereafter also caught on in Canada.

5. The Plautdietsch word for peaches is "Pirsche(n)." It was used in America until the 1920's when the immigrants brought with them the word "Pfirsichen" or "Firsichen" (as often mispronounced). It is the German name for peaches, adopted by them in Russia. Today one finds few Mennonites who even remember that peaches were called "Pirschen," or "Pirsche" in the Molotschna manner.

The foregoing five words are only a few of many adopted from the Russian, Ukrainian and German languages into Plautdietsch by Mennonites in Russia during the 1870-1920 period. These words and others similarly adopted were relatively unknown to immigrants of the 1870's to America; certainly they were not part of their normal daily speech.

Other Russian words such as "Arbus" (watermelon), "Bockelzhonn" (tomato) and "Vareniki" (cheese fritters, "perogy") had been adopted by Mennonites in Russia before 1870 because Plautdietsch apparently had no words for these new items in their diet. Other Russian words such as

"Droschki" (three-horse carriage), "Knaut" (rope) and "Schemmedaun" (clothing trunk) had also become known, and were adopted before 1870, and were consequently well known in America.

OTHER PRONUNCIATIONAL VARIANTS

A number of the variations in the Plautdietsch of Mennonites can be described as characteristics of either the Old or the New Colonies in Russia (Chortitza and Molotschna). But, the complexity of the matter does not allow such simple conclusions. Some variations fall within time frames, and might not have been prevalent in both colonies, as shall be discussed later.

Note: Readers will note that certain speech variations evident among speakers of Plautdietsch are not pursued here. The reasons are that they are so many, their current usages so intermixed, their origins so obscure that at this juncture in Plautdietsch history, it is questionable that they can be traced or whether it is of particular consequence whether they are traced. Nevertheless, a few shall be mentioned, as follows:

English	As it may be said in Plautdietsch
to bloom	blieeje, bleeje, bläje + (n)
to dry	drieeje, dreeje, dräje + (n)
to fly	flieeje, fleeje, fläje + (n)
to cook	koke, koake, koaken, köaken
to make	moke, moake, moaken, möaken
today	vondoog, vondoag, vondöag
would you?	wuddsd, wurzhd, wurdsd Du?
go to sleep	e'schlopen, enschlope
unashamed, unabashed	o'veschämt, onveschämt
you could, can	Du kunnst, ku'st, kaunst, kau'st
often	foake, foaken, föaken, oft
never again	nie mea, nie wada, nimmamea
I	ekj, etj
(I) came	kjeem, tjeem, kaum
(I) ate	eet, aut
on the whole	äwaheipt, äwahaupt
exactly	jeneiw, jenau

Change is inevitable in any language over decades or generations. So it was and continues to be with the Plautdietsch of the Mennonites. Assimilation and adoption of Russian, Ukrainian and German loan words and expressions inevitably took place in both major colonies and in their daughter colonies in Russia, particularly after exposure to them was increased in the educational system.

Due to current lack of authoritative information on spoken Plautdietsch in time periods before and after 1870, the following attempt to allocate a few of the variations in speech to their respective colonies and to applicable time periods runs some risk of errors and exceptions. On the other hand, some characteristics of speech as listed confirm that time periods are valid and essential parameters in describing variations in Plautdietsch.[80]

Speech Variations in Colony and Time Period

Characteristic of Speech	Colony (Chortitza)	(Molotschna)	Before 1870 (Period One)	1870 - 1920 (Period Two)
heiwe, bleiw keiwe		X	X	
haue, blau kaue		X		X
heiwen, bleiw keiwen	X		X	X
Leahrasche	X	X	X	
Lehrerin	X	X		X
Kjoakj, Kjäakj	X	X	(dominant)	(some)
Tjoatj, Tjäatj	X	X	(some)	(dominant)
Banj, Ritsch Knaut, Wareniki	X	X	X	X
Jehaun, Lena Kjnals, Käte	X	X	X	
Wanja, Ljolja Kornuusch, Katja	X	X		X
Retzen, Däaren gohnen, moaken	X		X	X
Retze, Däare gohne, moake		X	X	X
Dü, Hüs, büte	X		X	X
Du, Hus, bute		X	X	X

Summary of Chapter Seven

The netherlandic Mennonites had substantially abandoned their use of Dutch in worship and in writing when they settled in Russia after two and one half centuries in Prussia. Their day-to-day speech was in the Nether Prussian of the Vistula delta. In worship and in writing, some had begun to use a form of High German.

The dialectical mix of Low German adopted in Prussia and carried with them to Russia in the first two major migrations determined speech variations among them that eventually became known as the Old Colony (Chortitza) and New Colony (Molotschna) subdialects, with in-colony variations. Their spoken word as well as their language of worship and schooling during their first several decades in Russia were mostly Low German. Some writing and preaching was done in an impoverished and archaic form of High German by a few. The Russian and Ukrainian language were neither widely known nor used.

When the Mennonites arrived in Russia in 1789 and later, neither they nor their neighbours regarded them as German colonists. They looked upon themselves as "Dietsch," which could mean either Dutch or Low German. Their school reforms and Russian government reforms brought about greater use and acceptance among them of the High German language.

A half century after the Molotschna settlement began, another similar but somewhat smaller resettlement migration from West Prussia to the region of the Volga river began in 1853. Because of the great distance between the Volga settlements and the earlier Chortitza and Molotschna colonies, their dialectical differences had little effect upon the settlers of the older two colonies. And since descendants of the Volga settlers did not reach America in the numbers of those from the first two colonies, their language differences remained relatively unknown in America.

After 1870 the Russian government imposed reforms that forced Mennonites and other colonists to teach and use the Russian language. Another Russian reform at first cancelled Mennonite military exemptions, but then was modified to accommodate alternate civilian forestry service. One third of the Mennonites in Russia chose not to accept this reform and moved to Canada and the United States. Those who remained, countered increasing use of the Russian language with intensified use of German. A beneficial result of this increased education in languages was that Mennonites in Russia became fluent in both German and Russian.

The influence of Russian, Ukrainian and German upon spoken Low German in Russia during the period after 1870 gradually brought about changes in their spoken tongue, thus dividing Old Colony and New Colony subdialects into pre-1870 and post-1870 era divisions. In America, when migrants from Russia arrived after 1920, their speech-variant assimilations of the post-1870 era, along with more progressive attitudes, became differences which separated Rußlända or Russlända and Kanaudja (in Canada) and Amerikauna (in the States).

The chapter does not attempt to categorize characteristics of speech acquired since 1920, nor those that have developed in the spoken word of Mennonites in the seventy years before 1993 under influences of national languages in various countries.

The Plautdietsch mother tongue of netherlandic Mennonites is a Nether Prussian dialect of the Lower Saxon branch of Low German, laced with loan words from other languages and dialects.

NOTES TO CHAPTER SEVEN

Note: See Notes to Chapter One for Abbreviations

1. Although the area known as the Ukraine in which the first major Mennonite colonies were established, is often referred to by them as South Russia, at the time of those settlements they were located on lands newly conquered by Russia, and were then known as New Russia. See James Urry's *None but Saints*, pp. 51, 68, 70.

2. Walter Quiring, *Die Mundart von Chortitza in Süd-Rußland,* Inaugural Dissertation, (München: Druckerei Studentenhaus, Universität München, 1928) p. 46.
   —Jack Thiessen, "Origins of the Variations in Mennonite Plautdietsch," *MQR*, July, 1988, p. 290.

3. James Urry, "From Speech to Literature," p. 237.

4. *Ibid.*, p. 291.

5. Artur Gabrielsson, "Die Verdrängung der mnd. durch die nhd. Schriftsprache," *NSL*, pp. 145-146.

6. David G. Rempel, "The Mennonite Commonwealth in Russia," *MQR*, Vol. XLVII, October 1973, Number Four, p. 261.
   —James Urry, *None But Saints*, (Hyperion Press, 1989), p. 153. Urry states that although Mennonites emphasized the importance of literacy so that all could read the Bible, in reality most Mennonites could only stumble through (*German*) written material.
   —Quiring, p. 47.

7. David G. Rempel, "The Mennonite Commonwealth in Russia," *MQR*, Vol. XLVII, October 1973, p. 262, and Vol. XLVIII, January 1974, p. 40.
   —James Urry, *None But Saints*, (Hyperion Press, 1989), p. 161.

8. Rempel, *MQR*, October 1973, p. 262.

9. Rempel, "The Mennonite Commonwealth. . . ," *MQR*, October 1973, p. 260.

10. James Urry, "The Russian State, the Mennonite World . . . ," *Mennonite Life*, March 1991, p. 12.

11. James Urry, *None But Saints*, pp. 93,97. Urry states, "as early as 1806 Richelieu had noted that the Mennonites are astonishing, the Bulgarians incomparable, and the Germans intolerable."
    "From Speech to Literature," p. 239
    —Rempel, *MQR*, Oct. 1973, p. 295.
    —The way Mennonites of Prussia regarded their nationality at the time of their move into Russia, and the way they and others regard themselves today shows an interesting change. It is now common for Mennonites from Russia to regard themselves as German Mennonites, with which the German government agrees and on which the "Heimkehrer" policy of support for "returnees" from the USSR is based. Among those Mennonites who did not make the trek to Russia, but remained in Prussia (until 1945), the feeling of "Germanness" is also dominant. This is evident in an article in "Der Bote," 23 Sept. 1992, Nr. 35, in which a former Prussian Mennonite now living in Germany writes of a visit to the former homeland, and felt it necessary to explain as follows: "Wenn die Polen heute vorzugsweise von den 'holländischen Mennoniten' im Weichseldeltasprechen, so ist das historisch nicht unrichtig, . . . Andererseits fühlen sich Mennoniten aus dieser Gegend, . . . eindeutig als Deutsche."

12. Rempel, *MQR*, 1973, p. 262.

13. Rempel, *MQR*, 1974, p. 40.

14. *Ibid.*, 1974, p. 9.

15. *Ibid.*, p. 41.

16. *Ibid.*, p. 42.

17. Thiessen, *MQR*, July, 1988, p. 285.

18. Quiring, pp. 13, 42.
    —Thiessen, "Variations in Mennonite Plautdietsch," *MQR*, July, 1988, p. 285.

19. Quiring, pp. 2-3, Note #3.

20. Walter Ziesemer, *Die Ostpreußischen Mundarten*, (Wiesbaden: Dr. Maertin Sändig oHG., 1970), p. 137.

21. For more detailed and expanded information on the numbers of settlers and total populations at various time in the Chortitza, Molotschna and Volga Colonies, consult (among others) the following sources:
—*Mennonite Encyclopedia*, Vol. IV, pp. 381-388.
—Rempel, *MQR*, October 1973, pp. 293-294, 306-308.
—Unruh, *Die niederländisch-niederdeutschen Hintergründe . . .*, pp. 213-232.
—Urry, *None but Saints*, pp. 145, 285-298.

22. Quiring, p. 42.

23. Rempel, *MQR*, Oct. 1973, p. 291.

24. Rempel, "Russian Mennonite Commonwealth," *MQR*, October 1973, p. 291.

25. C. Henry Smith, *The Story of the Mennonites. 4th Edition*, (Newton: Mennonite Publishing House, 1957), p. 387.
—*Mennon. Encycl.*, "Chortitza Mennonite Settlement," Cornelius Krahn, (Scottdale: Mennonite Publishing House, 1959), p. 569.
—Quiring, pp. 9-13, p. 25.
—Jack Thiessen, "Origins of Variations in Mennonite Plautdietsch," *MQR*, July, 1988, p.288. Thiessen draws on information from Mannhardt to elaborate on the districts of the Vistula delta from which the Chortitza settlers originated. Some scholars do not mention that 20 families of the Chortitza settlers came from Elbing.

26. Horst Gerlach, "Von Westpreußen nach Rußland 1789-1989," *Westpreußen Jahrbuch*, Band 41, 1991, p. 104.

27. Quiring, p. 62.
—Jack Thiessen, *MQR*, July, 1988, p. 285.

28. Quiring, pp. 74-75.

29. *Ibid.*, pp. 74-75.

30. *Ibid.*, p. 54.

31. *Ibid.*, pp. 68-69.
—Jack Thiessen, *MQR*, July, 1988, p. 286.

32. Quiring, p. 60.
—Jack Thiessen, *MQR*, July, 1988, p. 288.

33. Unruh, p. 208.
—Smith, p. 397.

34. Rempel, "Russian Mennonite Commonwealth," *MQR*, October 1973, p. 306.

35. Smith., p. 397.
—Quiring, p. 16.

36. Jack Thiessen, "Mennoniten Plautdietsch, Woher? Wohin?" *Der Bote*, Nr. 14, 1. April 1992, p. 4.
—Thiessen, *MQR*, July, 1988, p. 294.

37. James Urry, "From Speech to Literature," p. 237.

38. *Ibid.*, p. 294.

39. Unruh, p. 231.

40. *Ibid.*, p. 401.
—*Mennon. Encycl.*, "Volga German Autonomous SSR," Vol. 4, p. 844.

41. *Journal of Mennonite Studies*, Vol. 5,1987, p. 149.

42. *Mennonite Encyclopedia*, "Galicia," Vol. 11, p. 435.

43. *Mennon. Encycl.,* "Volhynia," Vol. 4, p. 844.
—Smith, p. 400.

44. Rempel, *MQR,* January, 1974, pp. 24-30.

45. P.M. Friesen, p. 205.

46. *Ibid.,* pp. 395 & 469.

47. Rempel, *MQR,* January, 1974, pp. 9 & 35.

48. Rempel, *MQR,* October, 1973, pp. 282-286.

49. Rempel, *MQR,* October, 1973, p. 303.

50. *Ibid.,* pp. 263 & 295.

51. James Urry, *None But Saints,* Appendix 1, pp. 282-4.
—P. M. Friesen, *Mennonite Brotherhood,* pp. 119-20.

52. Rempel, *MQR,* Jan. 1974, p. 36.

53. *Ibid.,* p. 35, 42.

54. James Urry, *None But Saints,* p. 211.

55. Rempel, *MQR,* Jan. 1974, p. 36.
—James Urry, *None But Saints,* p. 215. Urry states that between 1873 and 1884 between 12,000 and 15,000 Mennonites left New Russia for the United States and Canada.
—Smith, *Story of the Mennonites,* p. 294. Smith states that by 1880 about 10,000 had left for the United States and about 8,000 for Manitoba.
—*Mennon. Encycl.* Vol. 111, p. 685. (18,000).

56. W.W. Moelleken, "Die Rußlanddeutschen Mennoniten in Kanada und Mexico," *Zeitschrift für Dialektologie und Linguistik. LIV. Jahrgang. Heft 2,* (Stuttgart: Franz Steiner Verlag Wiesbaden, 1987), p. 151.

57. Henry D. Dyck, *Language Differentiation in Two Low German Groups in Canada,* A *Dissertation,* University of Pennsylvania, Ph.D., 1964.

58. Urry suggests 20,000.

59. *Mennon. Encycl.,* "Migrations of Mennonites," Vol. 111, p. 685, (25,000 total) James Urry suggests 20,000.

60. *Ibid.,* Vol. 111, p. 685.

61. Rempel, *MQR,* January, 1974, p. 40.
—*Mennon. Encycl.,* "Johann Cornies," Vol. 1, p. 717.

62. Rempel, *MQR,* January, 1974, pp. 41-42.

63. Rempel, *MQR,* January 1974, p. 52.

64. Arnold Dyck, *Wellkaom op'e Forstei!,* (North Kildonan: Self Publication, 1950).

65. Joachim Born, Sylvia Dickgießer, *Deutschsprachige Minderheiten,* (Mannheim: Institut fur deutsche Sprache, 1989),p. 124. The authors quote Dr. Wolfgang W. Moelleken (1987) in his "Die rußlanddeutschen Mennoniten in Kanada und Mexico" in: Zeitschrift fur Dialektologie und Linguistik, H. 2., Wiesbaden, S. 145-183, as follows: "Neben dem Dialekt wird im begrenztem Umfang eine in Rußland gelernte Variante des Hochdeutschen gesprochen, die sich nach Moelleken deutlich vom 'üblichen' unterscheidet."

66. W.W. Moelleken, "Die Russlandeutschen Mennoniten," pp. 155-157.

67. W.W. Moelleken, "Sprachunterhaltungsfaktoren in den Mexikanischen Siedlungen der rußlanddeutschen Mennoniten, *Germanistische Mitteilungen 24 / 1986,* p. 69.

68. Jack Thiessen, *Predicht fier Haite,* (Hamburg: Helmut Buske Verlag, 1984). Thiessen is a Canadian-born Mennonite, educated at the University of Marburg in Germany. In the aforementioned book he lampoons Mennonite High German mercilessly, as the title suggests.

69. Unruh, p. 82.

70. Gilbert de Smet, "Niederländische Einflüsse im Niederdeutschen," *NSL,* pp. 739-740.

71. Dieter Möhn, "Geschichte der neuniederdeutschen Mundarten," *NSL,* pp. 163-164.

72. Dieter Stellmacher, *Niederdeutsch—Formen und Forschungen,* (Tübingen: Max Niemeyer Verlag , 1981), p. 112 .
—Penner, p. 180.
—Stellmacher, *NS,* p. 137.

73. Jack Thiessen, "The Low German of the Canadian Mennonites," *Mennonite Life*, July 1967, p. 110.

74. W.W. Moelleken, "Die linguistische Heimat der rußlanddeutschen Mennoniten in Kanada und Mexiko," 1987, p. 92. "Außerdem konnte ich im Jahre 1981 Tonbandaufnahmen von Sprechern in ausgesuchten Orten des Weichseldeltas durchführen, die sich als sehr aufschlußreich fur die Fixierung des Sprachlichen Ursprungs der rußlanddeutschen Mennoniten herausgestellt haben."
—Wicherkiewicz, Tomasz, "Sporen van de Mennonieten in Noord-Polen," *De taal der Mennonieten,* (Groningen: Vakgroep Taalwetenschap, Rijksuniversiteit Groningen, 1992), p. 25. "Helaas leverde mijn veldonderzoek in 1991 geen positieve uitkomst op. Ik heb geen Mennoniet gevonden die nu nog in Noord-Polen leeft. De enige nog in leven zijnde Mennoniet in Polen schijnt to zijn Franz Thgahrt uit Poznan..."

75. Walter Quiring, *Die Mundart von Chortitza un Süd-Rußland,* (Munchen: Druckerie Studentenhaus Munchen, Universität, 1928).
—W. W. Moelleken, "Die Linguistische Heimat der Rußlandeutschen Mennoniten in Kanada und Mexico," *Niederdeutsches Jahrbuch. Jahraang 1987,* p. 92.
Note: There was an earlier dissertation by J. Regehr published in Königsberg in 1902. However, it concentrated on the language as spoken by Mennonites in Prussia. It is quoted by Quiring.

76. Rempel, *MQR,* January 1974, p. 24.

77. Henry D. Dyck, *Language Differentiation in Two Low German Groups in Canada,* (Dissertation, 1964, University of Pennsylvania), p. 14.

78. Thiessen, *MQR,* July, 1988, p. 286
—Tolksdorf, *Danzig in acht Jahrhunderten,* (Munster: Nicolaus-Copernicus-Verlag, 1985), p. 322.

79. Thiessen, *Mennonite Low German Dictionary,* (Marburg: N.G. ElwertVerlag, 1977), p. Xll.

80. 1. Due to the dialectical mix among Mennonites in both major colonies in Russia, it is quite impossible, and not to be expected that classifying and ascribing speech characteristics to any colony at any particular time can be totally and exclusively reliable. Those variants that are usually thought of as being at home in the Chortitza Colony might also be heard among some speakers of the Molotschna Colony, and vice versa. Consequently, the classifications attempted here are not 100% reliable, nor can they be, but are simply indicators of trends as they then prevailed. Variations in Plautdietsch are found among Mennonites in any group or colony today. This has led scholars to remark that "the family is the smallest unit retaining speech realizations" (Jack Thiessen quoting Wolfgang Moelleken (Zeitschrift für Mundartforschung, 34, 1967, p. 251). As a matter of fact, even families are not necessarily dialectical units when the father and mother are from backgrounds of different subdialect, which is not uncommon.
2. Due to the complexity of classifying variations in spoken Plautdietsch, no attempt is here made to even generalize after 1920. Certainly we must expect that significant changes have taken place in the further 70 years that have elapsed since then, under such diverse influences as the Russian, English, German and Spanish languages in different parts of the Soviet Union, Germany. The United States and Canada, and Mexico and Paraguay, to name but a few of the major settlement areas.

CHAPTER EIGHT

The Status of Low German Today

Several "micro-censuses" conducted in northern Germany in the years 1963 and 1965 revealed that approximately fifty-one percent of the people of the city of Hamburg and sixty-seven percent of the people of Schleswig-Holstein regularly spoke Low German among friends and family.[1] These figures were repeatedly questioned, but they continued to prove that Low German constituted a substantial segment of language spoken in northern West Germany during the 1960's.

INSTITUTE FOR LOW GERMAN

These results confirmed that the Low German language was a major component of the social and working lives of people in northern Germany, great enough to justify the founding of an umbrella organization to nurture the language and to foster its cultural activities. Subsequently, with participation by the government of Germany, regional government representatives, University Professors and language specialists, along with well known Low German authors, a council was formed to found an "Institut für niederdeutsche Sprache" (Institute for the Low German language). The Institute was founded and its objectives formulated in meetings of the founding council during the years 1972 and 1973:

a. The Institute was to strive to meet practical needs for the nurture and use of the Low German language, without necessarily limiting itself to functions within the abilities of personnel or financial capabilities of the Institute. Over and above those projects which the Institute would carry out on its own, it was intended to assist, stimulate, support, coordinate and publicize Low German cultural activities carried on by other organizations.

b. Among projects to be initiated and undertaken by the Institute itself, its first objectives were to analyze, describe and record the status of Low German as it then existed, without prejudicing reference to the past.

Progress toward these objectives required that key activities would be to establish a library and archives of literature, reference books, statistical and general information on activities, such as the publication of Low German literature.

Survey of Speakers of Low German
in Germany

A survey was undertaken under auspices of the Institut für niederdeutsche Sprache in 1984 to determine, among other things, how many people in West Germany still spoke Low German and to what extent. The pertinent results of that survey were reported in a 1987 booklet "Wer spricht Platt?" (Who speaks Low German?) by Dieter Stellmacher. He reported that in northern West Germany alone there were at that time 5.6 million people who spoke Low German well to very well,[2] in addition to those who spoke it less well or poorly, or who understood it but did not speak it. When the 1984 figures are compared with those of twenty years earlier, they are seen to be about four to five percentage points higher. Stellmacher cautions that the higher figures do not necessarily indicate an increase in the number of speakers, but more probably stability in their numbers. That is so because increased tolerance toward Low German in today's society encourages more interviewees to admit that they speak it than would have done so twenty years earlier.

SPEAKERS OF LOW GERMAN
WORLD WIDE

Since the Low German language is now removed from its former position of far-reaching commercial and diplomatic prominence of five centuries ago, it no longer commands a high public profile. Consequently, when discussing the Low German language among those who know it as mother tongue, it is understandably commonplace to hear the question, "How many people still speak Low German?" The following statistics attempt to answer that question.

SOURCES OF STATISTICS

The sources of information on numbers of speakers of Low German in various countries as listed hereinafter are as follows:

— "Wer Spricht Platt?" (Who Speaks Low German?) by Dieter Stellmacher, published by Institut für niederdeutsche Sprache, Bremen 1, 1987.

—"Ethnologue", Eleventh edition, 1988, "The Languages of the World" published by the Summer Institute of Linguistics, Inc., Dallas, Texas.

—Mennonitische Umsiedlerbetreuung (Mennonite Émigré Service Centre), Neuwied, Germany, 1992.

—"Deutschsprachige Minderheiten", (German Speaking Minorities), by Joachim Born and Sylvia Dickgießer, published by Institut für deutsche Sprache, Mannheim, 1989.

Countries and Speakers
of Low German

Country	Source of Information	Number of Speakers
Argentina	Ethnologue, 1988, quotes Kloss and McConnell report of 1978, speakers of Mennonite Plautdietsch	140
Belize	Ethnologue, 1988, speakers of Mennonite Plautdietsch (7,440)[3]	5,140
Bolivia	Ethnologue, 1988, speakers of Mennonite Plautdietsch (Est. 1985)	18,000
Brazil	Ethnologue, 1988, speakers of Mennonite Plautdietsch (Est. 1985)	5,955
Canada	Ethnologue, 1988, quotes Kloss and McConnell report of 1978, speakers of Mennonite Plautdietsch[4]: as first language as second language	80,000 20,000
C.I.S. (former USSR)	1992 Umsiedlerbetreuung (estimate)[5] Plautdietsch only — minimum — — maximum —	(17,500) (20,000)
Costa Rica	Ethnologue, 1988, quotes report by Minnich, 1974, Plautdietsch	100
Germany (East)	—No published figures available[6] See below for (tentative) estimates: (Tentative) calculation based on extrapolating West German figures: 1979 pop. West Germany—62,827,000 1979 pop. East Germany —16,716,000	?
Germany (East)	(Extrapolated) total of speakers of Low German in 1979 East Germany 16,716/62,827 x 5,600,000[7] =	(1,489,500)
Germany (West)	—Figures from "Wer Spricht Platt," Multi-dialect exc. Plautdietsch	5,600,000

| Germany (West) | —Estimates from Umsiedlerbetreuung,[8] | |
| | Mennonite Plautdietsch only, 1992 | 60,000 |

Mexico *	Deutschsprachige Minderheiten, 1989,	
	Mennonite Plautdietsch	40,000
	Ethnologue, 1988, estimate of 1983	42,000
	W.W. Moelleken 1986, quotes Walter	
	Schmiedehaus, 1982	60,000

| Netherlands | No published figures available | ? |
| | See below for (estimate): | |

(Considering	1988 pop.—Groningen	556,757
provinces of	1988 pop.—Drenthe	436,586
Groningen,	1988 pop.—Overijssel	1,009,997
Drenthe,	Total pop. (3 Prov.)	2,003,340
Overijssel	Assuming that 25%[9] of the people	
only)[10]	in these provinces speak Low Saxon,	
	speakers of Low Saxon (estimated)	(500,000)

Paraguay*	Ethnologue, 1988, Figures from MBC	
	1986, Plautdietsch only	38,000
	Deutschsprachige Minderheiten, 1989,	
	Mennonite Plautdietsch (for 1987)	22,710

| Uruguay | Ethnologue, 1988, Plautdietsch only | 1,200 |

U.S. of America	—Ethnologue, 1988, quotes Kloss and	
	McConnell report of 1978. Speakers	
	of Mennonite Plautdietsch	10,000

Estimated world-wide *total* number of speakers of Low German, from tallies of the foregoing information—
All dialects: —Maximum 7,908,000
—Minimum 7,850,210

Estimated world-wide *total* number of speakers of Mennonite Low German from foregoing information—
Plautdietsch dialect only—Maximum 318,500
—Minimum 260,710

*Disparities in figures for Mexico and Paraguay are noted and included in minimum and maximum totals.

The foregoing figures conservatively indicate that Low German speakers around the world number nearly eight (7.9) million. These figures are probably modest, considering that they do not include speakers of Low German in Belgium, Denmark and Poland or the considerable number in Canada and the United States[11] who speak dialects other than Mennonite Plautdietsch. Of the eight million total, just over seven million (approx. 7,149,500) live in Germany.

Plautdietsch speakers probably number fewer than three hundred thousand, about 3.8% among speakers of Low German world wide. About sixty thousand of them currently (1992) live in Germany where they have in recent years resettled from Russia.

Current Scholastic and Literary Activities in Low German in Europe

Since more than seven million of the world's population of speakers of Low German live in Germany, it is understandable that the great majority of scholastic and literary activities in the language would take place there. However, the healthy state of Low German in Germany also reflects a general social enlightenment fostering openness toward and appreciation of dialect literature, including Low German. This is not the case among all Low German people nor world wide, as touched upon later in this chapter.

LOW GERMAN LITERATURE IN THE MARKETPLACE

The Institut für niederdeutsche Sprache gathers information on Low German literature available in the bookstores. Their publication "Plattdeutsch im Buchhandel" (Low German in the Bookmarket) for 1991[12] lists some seventeen hundred Low German titles currently available, and acknowledges that some publications have not yet been recorded. Those titles listed are the works of over eight hundred authors published by some three hundred publishers. Authors are individually listed by name, and publishers by name and address.

Low German literature published and available in bookstores in Germany today takes many forms, including: novels, books of stories, books of poems, books of humor, song books, hymn books, devotional materials, dictionaries, magazines, calendars, almanacs, yearbooks, stage productions, records and cassette recordings.

LITERARY SOCIETIES AND ASSOCIATIONS

Many communities in northern Germany and the Netherlands have local literary societies which foster and enjoy Low German literature, drama, singing or other forms of literary activities. Each of these societies serves a local need and is active in a local dialect. They are scattered throughout the Low-German-speaking region.

With financial support of the province of Nether Saxony and various local and city governments, an annual three-day literary conference called "Bevensen Tagung" is held in October in the city of Bad Bevensen

105

on Lüneburger Heide, south of Hamburg. It is attended by Low German authors, publishers, scholars and others interested in Low German cultural activities.

LOW GERMAN RADIO BROADCASTING IN GERMANY

As of 1983, radio NDR of Hamburg recorded a regular radio listening audience of a million listeners to their Low German programming, with occasional listeners boosting this number to over two million. To these must be added listeners to Radio Bremen and WDR of Münster, also broadcasting in Low German at that time.

In August of 1992, Radio NDR "Norddeutscher Rundfunk"[12] reported regular programming schedules as follows:
—exclusively Low German—*)
—partially Low German—#)

NDR 1 Welle Nord. Abt. "Heimat u. Kultur":
(NDR 1 Wave North, "Home and Culture" Div.):

Monday,	20.05 Uhr (8:05 pm)	*)	"Bökerschapp" (Bookcase), Low German for Monday evening, (55 minutes)
Wednesday,	20.05 Uhr (8:05 pm)	#)	"Von Binnenland und Waterkant" From Inland and Coastline), the Home Magazine, (55 minutes)
Friday,	20.05 Uhr (8.05 pm)	#)	"Bi uns to Huus" (At home with us) Everyday commentary from Schleswig-Holstein, (55 minutes)
Mon.-Sat.,	8.50 Uhr (8:50 am)	*)	"Hör mal 'n beten to" (Listen for a moment) Low German morning Chat, (2 1/2 minutes)
Monday,	20.30Uhr (8:30 pm)	*)	"Die plattdeutsche Geschichte" (The Low German Story) From listeners to listeners of "Bookcase" (5 minutes)
Thursday,	8.15 Uhr (6:15 pm)	*)	"Die plattdeutsche Glosse" in "Kultur Kompakt" (The Low German Commentary in Culture Compact)
Five times annually		*)	"Ünner't Strohdack" (Under Thatched Roof) public Low German readings in open air theatre, (90 minutes)
Once annually		*)	"Fleitjepiepen" (The Flutes) A Low German Talkshow (115 minutes)

Additionally, on Channel NDR 4:

Saturday,	20.05 Uhr *) (8:05 pm)	"Niederdeutsches Hörspiel" (Low German Radio Play), broadcasts alternate with "Niederdeutsche Chronik" (Low German Chronicle) History of North German civilization
Five times annually, on Holidays	#)	"Zwischen Ems und Oder" (Between the Ems and Oder rivers),Weekdays in northern Germany

NDR 1 Radio Niedersachsen:
(NDR 1 Radio Lower Saxony):

Monday,	20.05 Uhr *) (8.05 pm)	"Plattdeutsch am Montagabend" (Low German on Monday evening) (55 minutes)

NDR 1 Hamburg Welle:
(NDR 1 Hamburg Frequency):

Sunday,	18.30 Uhr (6:30 pm)	80 Minutes of Low German, once every four weeks

NDR 1 Radio Mecklenburg/Vorpommern:
(NDR 1 Northern [former] East Germany):

Sunday,	8.05 Uhr (8:05 am)	"Up Platt" (In Low German) (55 minutes)

The Low German Radio broadcast heard by most listeners is the "Hör mal 'n beten to" program which is a short, Monday-to-Saturday morning broadcast, with listening audiences of from 1.1 to 1.3 million people. Evening programming, being more specialized in nature, draws a listening audience of some forty to eighty thousand in Hamburg and Schleswig-Holstein.

Radio Bremen and Radio WDR Münster also enjoy sizable audiences listening to their regional programming.

LOW GERMAN SCHOLASTIC ACTIVITIES
IN EUROPE

Among items of major interest connected with the study of Low German is the fact that, in West Germany alone, the following four universities have established chairs of Low German studies:

1. Göttingen[14]
2. Hamburg[15]
3. Kiel[16]
4. Münster[17]

In addition to the aforementioned chairs of Low German studies, other universities in Bielefeld, Marburg, Oldenburg, Rostock and Greifswald employ professors with Low German as a specialty. In the University of Groningen in the Netherlands, one professor[18] specializes in the Nether Saxon language, while at least one colleague[19] is currently actively engaged (1991-1992) in pursuing the study of Plautdietsch among Mennonites in Siberia, along with other language assignments.

Within enlightened circles in Europe today, positively appreciative attitudes prevail in places where they were formerly derogatory. Universities actively engage in study and research, gathering and publishing information on Low German in its various dialects, including Mennonite Plautdietsch. Correspondence from some professors indicates that they are indeed well informed of Mennonites and their Low German. In an article on the history of Low German dialects,[20] Dieter Möhn of the University of Hamburg refers to the Low German Mennonites as worthy representatives of the world-language Low German.

Numerous research and reference textbooks on various aspects of the subject "Low German" have been written by the aforementioned professors and scholars. A number of such books are identified in the notes and bibliography to this story. The foremost of these (the most "wissenschaftlich") at this time is probably "Handbuch zur niederdeutschen Sprach- und Literaturwissenschaft" (Handbook of Scholastic Knowledge of the Language and Literature of Low German) by Gerhard Cordes and Dieter Möhn.

The travels of Professor Tjeerd de Graaf of the University of Groningen in the Netherlands, incidental to a language research project in Asia, brought him into contact with Plautdietsch-speaking inhabitants of the Mennonite village of Neudachino, between Omsk and Novosibirsk, Siberia, with whom he visited. De Graaf was impressed with the similarity between the Plautdietsch spoken in Neudachino and the Low Saxon dialect of his Netherlandic home province of Groningen. He describes the Siberian encounter in a Dutch magazine article entitled, "In Siberië Spreken ze Grunnings," (In Siberia they speak [the dialect of Groningen]).

His report on his incidental discovery of Plautdietsch spoken among Mennonites in Siberia, together with a request for funding for more systematic and planned research, resulted in a grant from the University of Groningen to begin such a research project during the summer of 1992.

On the 24th of October 1992, the universities of Groningen and Oldenburg jointly convened a symposium in Groningen on the Plautdietsch dialect. It was attended by twenty-two scholarly participants from the Netherlands, Germany and Poland, including Professor Margarita Wall, formerly of Novosibirsk, now living in Germany. A 43-page report containing submissions to this one-day symposium was produced under the title, "De Taal der Mennoniten," (The Language of the Mennonites).

Current Scholastic and Literary Activities in Plautdietsch

Since the first doctoral dissertation on the Plautdietsch dialect in Russia by Jacob (Walter) Quiring in 1928, there have been several scholarly works dealing with other facets of the dialect. Apparently all of these works were done in or through non-Mennonite educational institutions.

The University of Winnipeg, central to Canada's netherlandic Mennonites, has a Chair of Mennonite Studies and a division known as Menno Simons College. Yet, these emphases appear not to include studies of the Low German language in which Menno Simons once wrote many of his works. It seems strange that a Canadian university with Mennonite emphases would not become involved in the study of Low German, when universities in Germany and in the Netherlands study even the Mennonite Plautdietsch dialect of Low German. This raises questions as to what motives might lie behind such noninvolvement.

THE PLAUTDIETSCH SHARE OF
LITERARY ACTIVITIES

Authors Harry Loewen and Al Reimer describe literary development in Canadian-Mennonite Low German in Mennonite Quarterly Review of 1985.[21] Their article provides a generous measure of positive information on literary activities in Plautdietsch.

The first Mennonite generally known to have published in Plautdietsch was J.H. Janzen, remembered for his playlet entitled "De Bildung" (Education), published in Russia in 1912, followed by "Daut Schultebott," (The Village Council) 1913, and "De Enbildung," (Pretensions) 1913. He continued his writing in Plautdietsch after immigrating to Canada in the 1920's.

For his first writings in Plautdietsch, Janzen had few existing guidelines. Until then, it had hardly been written. Possibly, he was not familiar with literature in other dialects of Low German for which spelling guidelines were by then evolving. But, he followed the example of the German language in phonetic system and alphabet for his writing in Plautdietsch. The wisdom of that choice has been amply confirmed by Low German orthographers. But, it appears that he had not come to grips with how to represent palatalized consonants. He seems to ignore them, and writes "eck," not "ekj" or "etj," and "keem" as opposed to "kjeem" or "tjeem." His writings also evidence the influences of High German in the Plautdietsch of his period in Russia. Words such as "oft," "nimmamea" and "Ruh" are High German infusions. Following is one of his better-known poems, apparently written in Canada:

"Plautdietsch"
von J.H. Janzen
1878-1950

Maunch eena kaun kjeen Plautdietsch mea	Some cannot speak Low German now
un schämt sikj nich eenmol:	and aren't a bit ashamed:
Em Jääjendeel, he meent sikj sea	Instead of that, they pride themselves
met siene huage School,	in schooling they have gained,
rädt Huagdietsch, Enjelsch, Russch—soo väl	speak German, English, Russian - yes,
daut eenem dieslich woat.	so much, it spins my mind.
Weat es de gaunze Kjlätamähl	Such claptrap is not even worth
nich een Schinkjeschwoat.	a paltry bacon rind.
Aus ekj noch kjleen wea, saut ekj oft	When I was small, I often sat
bi Mutta opp'e Schoot,	upon my mother's knee.
opp Plautdietsch säd se, — O, soo oft —	She'd say, "My boy, I love you so;
"Mien Jung, ekj si di goot!"	you mean so much to me!"
Waut Mutta Plautdietsch too mi säd,	What mother said in her own tongue,
daut klung soo woarm un tru,	that rang so warm and true;
daut ekj daut nimmamea vejät	that I shall nevermore forget
bat too de latzte Ruh.	until my final due.
(Slightly reworked by Reuben Epp)	(Freely translated by Reuben Epp

The next writer to enter the Plautdietsch literary scene in Canada was Arnold Dyck (1889-1970). He began publishing in Plautdietsch and in German in Manitoba in the 1940's after having arrived in Canada in the 1920's. The artistry of Dyck's numerous plays and stories proved that his writing skills in Mennonite Low German were without equal in his time. His words captured the essence of the Mennonite disposition, reflecting it in its variety and contradictions in the characters of his stories. His pencil sketches accompanying and illustrating his works proved him also to be an accomplished graphic artist.

Dyck's works did not receive their deserved acclaim during his lifetime. This resulted partly from his printing them in Fraktur (Old German or Gothic) lettering, using pronunciational symbols, at a time when that style was being replaced by Latin lettering as in English. Awareness among his potential readership of a resurgence in Low German literary activity was long overdue. A General disinterest and disrespect for its literature still lingered from a previous century. Ingrained Mennonite frugality restrained the "waste" of money on "nonessentials" such as secular books. During Dyck's lifetime, these factors combined to hamper widespread acceptance of his publications.

Fortunately, for posterity and for those now interested in Dyck's artistry, his works in Low German and in High German have been collected and reprinted under auspices of the Manitoba Mennonite

Historical Society as "Collected Works of Arnold Dyck, Vols. I, II, III & IV." His Plautdietsch stories and plays, edited by Al Reimer and rewritten with a changed spelling system in standard print, are contained in volumes II and III.

In 1982 at the University of Winnipeg, a one-day symposium of Low German authors and other interested persons was convened under the chairmanship of Al Reimer. Its purpose was to lay the groundwork for a standardized writing system for Plautdietsch. The points of the system, developed item for item at that meeting, were subsequently employed by Reimer in his editing of the works of Dyck. Herman Rempel's dictionary, published two year later, did not fully conform to that system, nor have the writings of others since then. No further symposia of that group have been held.

Additions to the Plautdietsch literary scene in printed form were two dictionaries, one by Jack Thiessen in 1977 and another by Herman Rempel in 1984. The seventy page work by Thiessen translates Plautdietsch words into German and English. The two hundred and ninety-five page work by Rempel translates Plautdietsch into English and English into Plautdietsch.

Among other Mennonite writers to have published works in Plautdietsch are Jacob Goerzen and Wm. Pauls of Alberta, Elisabeth and Victor Peters, N.H. Unruh, G.A. Peters and T.G. Klassen of Manitoba, Victor Carl Friesen of Saskatchewan and Reuben Epp of British Columbia. An avid interest in Plautdietsch stage performances is evident in the successes of the Landmark Theatre Group in southern Manitoba since the early 1980's. There is also a Low German singing group by the name of "Heischraitje & Willa Honich" (Locusts and Wild Honey) which has performed well in Manitoba and has published several recordings.

For a number of years Radio Southern Manitoba (CFAM) has broadcast Plautdietsch sermons by J.J. Neufeld of Winnipeg. Neufeld has retired and the work was taken over by Gerhard Friesen. During his years of radio ministry, Neufeld translated the New Testament into Plautdietsch, published in 1987 under the title "Daut Niehe Tastament."

As admirable as these literary activities in Plautdietsch may seem, such pursuits among about three hundred thousand speakers, when compared with those of seven to eight million speakers of other dialects, should have proportionately yielded some fifty to seventy resultant publications on bookstore shelves in 1991. In fact, Plautdietsch literature falls far short of the three to four percent share that might have been generated by its speakers, had they been as engaged in it as the rest of the Low German family.

Scholarly research or literary activities in Low German among Mennonites receive too little support in North America. This determines that whatever dialect literature is published derives its support largely from individual initiative. Unfortunately, its manner and style often evidences isolation from the influences of the quality to be found in works

111

such as those by Arnold Dyck and in literature written in other dialects of Low German.

Canadian and American Low German Mennonites probably have greater economic, educational and cultural possibilities for scholarly and literary engagement in Plautdietsch than do other Mennonites elsewhere.

In spite of not being noted for literary activities in their own dialect, netherlandic Mennonites and their tongue appear to receive more than their proportional share of scholastic attention in the universities of Europe.

DISTRIBUTION OF SPEAKERS AND LITERARY ACTIVITIES

It seems impossible to expect concerted literary activities among the widely-scattered thousands of speakers of Plautdietsch. Geographic isolation between settlements coupled with unfavorable economic conditions in some cases, and ultraconservative social outlooks among others, are not conducive to the pursuit of literary interests. Many of its speakers hold Low German in such low esteem that suggestions of reading, writing or studying it are disdained.

Germany and Russia. Among the world's speakers of Plautdietsch, about eighty to one hundred thousand now live in scattered locations in Germany and the former Soviet Union. Those who have recently emigrated from Russia are still adjusting to their new surroundings in Germany. Given their circumstances, it is unrealistic to expect that any new Low German literary interests might soon arise among them. Among speakers of Plautdietsch in Russia, it is unlikely that we could expect otherwise. It is unknown to what extent they harbour the negative perceptions described by Unruh some forty years ago when he said, "Low German was mistakenly but widely regarded by them as an inferior language."[22]

Latin America. About one hundred thousand speakers of Plautdietsch live in Latin America, from Mexico to Paraguay. Geographic distances and lack of communication among them do not foster literary exchange. Nor do their perceptions and economic status in many cases encourage such pursuits. Among the sizable Low German Mennonite population in Mexico, Moelleken[23] reports of his 1980's interviews that many regarded their spoken Low German as inferior. They believed that Low German could not be written because it had no alphabet. They also felt that it lacked culture. Such negative perceptions seem to be recycled versions of those described by Unruh forty years earlier. Those views, and their resultant negative attitudes toward Low German stem from lack of knowledge about the language and its literature.[24]

United States and Canada. Some eighty to one hundred thousand speakers of Mennonite Low German (Ethnologue figures) live primarily in farming communities scattered about the central and western United States and Canada and southern Ontario. A few urban concentrations similar to, but smaller than, that of the city of Winnipeg also exist. Any future increase in Low German literary activities among Mennonites most likely would be led by these in English-speaking America. Although scattered across the continent, travel and communication among them is not a serious problem. They have the progressiveness, openness toward education, freedom from want and availability of time to pursue scholastic and literary interests in Low German—to their own benefit and enjoyment. Those advantages enhance their ability to expand on literary beginnings made by J.H. Janzen and brought into fruition by Arnold Dyck.

LITERARY SHORTFALL IN PLAUTDIETSCH

The fact that literary activities in Plautdietsch are less than proportional to the number of its speakers may be at least partly attributable to the fact that speakers of Plautdietsch are scattered over numerous countries whereas about seven million speakers of other dialects are located in one country. However, geographic distances alone do not necessarily impact negatively upon literary pursuits, as is seen in a small community of about one thousand speakers of Low German in Cole Camp, Missouri. The community annually stages a Low German Theatre for several days. They also exchange theatrical visits with a similar group in Germany. Their dialect is that of the region between Bremen, Hamburg and Lüneburg. The enthusiasm of the Cole Camp group does not allow distances from other Low German groups to bar them from literary activities in Low German. They composed a history of their Low German community as well as video cassettes of their annual theatrical programs, which are for sale.

After a number of years of trying to obtain samples of Flemish dialect literature from various sources in Belgium, my efforts have not produced results. Bookstores in Belgium and Flemish people in Canada advise that although the Flemish speak their dialect at home in Flanders, they write only in Dutch. Dialect literature in Flanders is relatively unknown and unavailable because the Flemish people simply do not write in their Flemish dialect.

When this Flemish inhibition toward writing in their dialect is paired with the traditional absence of writing among Frisians, of whom Unruh has said that they were "not literary minded,"[25] we bring together two traits which, individually or coupled, inhibit or limit literary pursuits.

When we then consider that at the time of their beginnings, netherlandic Mennonites were a mix of Flemish and Frisian peoples, one could well expect to find among them traits and characteristics stemming from either or both of these forebears. Perhaps, today's Mennonites have inherited from their Flemish and Frisian ancestors those very traits which by their nature now hinder participation in literary activities in Plautdietsch.

Many Mennonite speakers of Low German may not realize that it is their mother tongue; that it dates back with them to the beginnings of the Anabaptist movement in the Netherlands at least four hundred and fifty years ago. Some of them erroneously believe that their mother tongue is High German, not knowing that the Frisian part of the Netherlands from whence they originated was not High German country. Menno Simons himself spoke and wrote in Low German and Dutch. As a native Frisian he, of course, mastered the Frisian language as well.

Some who know Low German as mother tongue do not necessarily perceive it as a heritage worth preserving. It is not uncommon among speakers of the Plautdietsch dialect of Low German to look upon this mother tongue with disrespect.[26]

THE IGNORANCE/DISRESPECT CYCLE

When a language is neither nurtured nor cared for, even its speakers do not become knowledgeable of it. For example: unschooled speakers of English in Canada, including those with fair mastery of the spoken word, often know little of its Anglo-Saxon or Germanic origins or its literature. Being able to speak or to write in English does not imply knowledge about the language, nor of its beauty or interrelationships with other languages.

Similarly, fluency in Plautdietsch does not necessarily indicate knowledge of it, much less about the Low German language as a whole. But, knowing about it and understanding its history, its beauty and its relationship to its mother language fosters respect and love for it and its family of dialects. That entails much more than just being able to speak it; knowledge of a language goes beyond the ability to manipulate its stock of words.

The eighteenth century was a period of discrimination against the dialects in Germany.[27] Low German was commonly thought of as a socially-limiting language of the lower stratum, from which the educationally-ambitious must hold themselves aloof. As late as 1924 Ziesemer[28] stated that in wide circles, even among the educated, an attitude prevailed that Low German was the sunken language of the plebs from which one must keep one's distance.

Professor Stellmacher points out in "Wer Spricht Platt?" that contempt for Low German results from ignorance of it. Of such attitudes, he says, "Daß das Niederdeutsche von denen gering geschätzt wird, die von ihm wenig wissen, überrascht nicht,"[29] (That Low German is held in contempt by those who are ignorant of it, is not surprising). He suggests that such ignorance be countered by teaching about the language at every opportunity.

It seems nowhere sufficiently emphasized that disrespect for Low German, which follows from ignorance of it, further inhibits the very learning that might banish that ignorance. The inevitable, ensuing consequence is that ignorance fosters disrespect, and disrespect fosters continued ignorance. Thus, the ignorance-disrespect cycle repeats, continues and repeats itself viciously from generation to generation without apparent end.

In nineteenth century Europe, the ignorance-disrespect cycle of centuries was finally halted by educated enlightenment fostered by changing social attitudes.[30] But, traditional conservative "isolation-from-the-world" tenets among Mennonites are not conducive to enlightenment in secular matters such as study of the spoken language. Even those with more liberal educations and broader social perspectives may be hampered by the contagion of common disrespect for their language. If so, they have not yet broken out of the cycle!

Literary Future of Plautdietsch in English-speaking America

Universities in Germany and the Netherlands devote faculty and financial resources to the study and research of Low German, including the Plautdietsch dialect of the Mennonites. How much more logical it would seem for the Mennonites themselves to be undertaking such research on Plautdietsch. It is, after all, their language, stemming from their netherlandic origins some four and one half centuries ago and still spoken among them.

PROUD FACTS

There are numerous reasons why speakers of Low German can be proud of their mother tongue, why they should strive to preserve it and its history, and why they should foster and nurture scholastic and literary activities in it. Those who are aware of those reasons are active in Low German literature and other literary activities.

Origin. The early history of English and Low German shows that they are sibling languages with a common Old Saxon parent. In the Middle Ages Low German held greater international rank than did English. Low German was the language of business in London's Steelyard, the trading enclave of the Hanseatic League in the heart of England at the time of Hanseatic greatness. Consequently, the origin of Low German ranks well alongside that of English.

Status. We know that the Plautdietsch dialect spoken by netherlandic Mennonites is a dialect of the Nether Saxon branch of Low German, more specifically, a member of the eastern Low German family of dialects, with Nether Prussian orientation. As such, it ranks among the best in Low German.

Literature. After centuries of prominence in the Middle Ages, followed by several centuries of obscurity, Low German enjoys a literary renaissance which began in the 1850's and still continues. Literary activity in Plautdietsch got started somewhat later (about 1912) and has not yet fully come into its own.

Writing System. Fairly good writing systems for Low German were developed by authors Groth and Reuter in the 1850's. A modern system was further refined and published under leadership of Johannes Saß in 1976. The new system applies (with some modifications) to all dialects of the language. It uses the standard Latin alphabet as in English and German, with umlauts as in German, and employs German phonetics. Although no "official" orthography for Low German exists, the Saß system is endorsed by most authors of Low German and is looked upon by scholars as "quasi-official" in rank.[31] Low German has a writing system![32] Its applicability and adaptability to Plautdietsch is demonstrated in the poetry samples that follow.

Refinement. Given a choice, some seek in a language that quality which they perceive as enabling them to project "refinement." This perception presupposes that a language, once selected for this quality from among others, confers refinement upon the words of the user or helps the speaker project an air of refinement when used. In fact, it seems more likely that a refined speaker (or writer) confers refinement upon the language he/she chooses to use by his/her refined manner of using that language.

Whatever is said or written in English or in German may project either refinement or vulgarity, depending upon how and by whom it is said or written. Both languages lend themselves well to the expression of either, as is also the case in Low German. When reading (on following pages) the poems, "Un Best et uk Nich" and "De Bua aun Siene Fru," the reader may judge whether the language used by these authors conveys "refinement" as written.

Expressiveness. The ability of Low German to communicate wholesome expressions is described in a passage from "Niederdeutsch Heute" in Chapter Four. The language lacks modern technical terminology, without doubt. But, its vocabulary of expressive terms and sayings probably goes unmatched by another language. It contains a richness in figures of speech unsurpassed by either German or English. In Low German one can express thoughts and feelings that in English or German leave one grasping for words of adequate expression.

Stability. The continuing stability and homogeneity of Plautdietsch are evident when one combines the following statements by two scholars:

Horst Penner[33] says of the Nether Saxon language as spoken in Groningen and Royal Prussia at the time of the sixteenth century Mennonite resettlement, "Die niedersächsische Mundart . . . wurde genauso in Groningen wie in Danzig gesprochen," (The Nether Saxon tongue was spoken in Groningen exactly as it was in Danzig). This indicates remarkable similarity in the language at that time between such widely-separated places as the Netherlands and Prussia.

Tjeerd de Graaf[34] says of it in 1992, after his visit among Mennonites between Omsk and Novosibirsk (in the CIS), "In Siberië spreken ze Grunnings," (In Siberia . . [the Mennonites] . . speak the dialect of Groningen). This comment attests to an amazing stability in the language as spoken in such diverse places as Siberia and

Groningen, even after its speakers in Siberia have been isolated from Groningen and its environs for more than four hundred years.

This overall consistency is further evident in that when speakers of the dialect meet, whether they are from America, from Russia or from Prussia, they converse as easily as picking up on yesterday's conversation. This uniformity continues despite their forefathers having gone separate ways two centuries ago.

Mother Tongue. One of the proudest qualities in Low German for netherlandic Mennonites is that it is their mother tongue wherever they live today. The Anabaptists of the Frisia Triplex spoke Low German at the time of Menno Simons, and they have continued to speak it with some dialectical change throughout four hundred and fifty years of history. Menno Simons was an educated person who spoke and wrote in Low German as well as Dutch.

If this story about Low German and Plautdietsch helps someone to better know about and to respect the Low German language and its Plautdietsch dialect, perhaps some love for them may ensue. Knowing about a language promotes better understanding of it. Furthermore, knowing and understanding Low German helps us in North America toward a better understanding of English.

Certainly, knowledge of Low German opens the door to enjoying hundreds of excellent books and other literature currently available in it. This language and mother tongue of the netherlandic Mennonites is worthy of preservation. It is a heritage. Now is the time to begin cherishing it.

AN EXAMPLE OF EAST FRISIAN HERITAGE

Many Low German Mennonites do not know that one of their greatest Low German authors was Wilhelmine Siefkes. She lived in Leer, East Friesland and wrote in her local East Frisian dialect of Low German. Since Mennonites of the Prussian-Russian-American contingent now lack familiarity with that dialect, albeit part of their former netherlandic heritage, they do not now easily read it. Consequently, one of her poems is here transcribed into easier-to-read Plautdietsch and appears hereafter:

The following poem "Un Best et uk Nich" was written by the Mennonite authoress and poetess Wilhelmine Siefkes in her native Low German dialect of East Friesland. It was first published in De plattdüütsch Klenner (Oldenburg) for the year 1966 under the title "Un büst't ok neet." With express written permission from Siefkes to rework and to further present this poem, it was transcribed from its original East Frisian dialect into Plautdietsch by Reuben Epp in 1974.

"Un Best et uk Nich"
von Wilhelmine Siefkes
Leer, Ostfriesland
(1890-1984)

Eenmol, du jingst nich mea aun Muttaschhaund,
   Rannsd du met korte Staupes derch een Gang
    Un stundst meteenst ver 'ne Jläsawaund
   Un sahgst een Kjind met Uage framd un bang.
Un daut weascht du. . . ,
                            un weascht et oba nich.

Du waundazhd derch de Welt, aus de Jugend mag,
   Joahrut, joahren, haudst Hunga un wordst saut.
    Du wachtsd hinja jieda Dreih, auf't Jleckj doa lag,
   Un fungst dien Nome un Bild opp Buak un Blaut.
Jo, daut weascht du. . . ,
                            un weascht et uk nich.

Wiet es dien Waig; de Sonn steiht hinja di,
   Doch eena jeiht noch ver di, schwoat un lang;
    Rannst du uk bi mauncheenem vebi,
   Disa moakt diene Staupe met, un jeiht dien Gang.
Uk daut best du. . . ,
                            un best et doch nich.

Weetst du dann, Menschekjind, wäm dit nu jellt . . . ?
   Doa steiht een Huus: sass Bräda haft sien Holt,
    Un dee doa wohnt, woat nich jefroagt auf't ahm jefällt;
   He liggt doa eensom, liggt doa stell un kolt.
Un daut best du. . . ,
                          doch, best et uk nich!

"And Yet, You Are it Not"

A version in English
of the poem
`Un büst't ok neet'
by Wilhelmine Siefkes

One time, no longer held by mother's hand,
   You ran with short steps down a hall
    And stopped before a glassy wall
   To see a child with eyes bewildered and afraid.
And that was you. . . ,
                       and yet, you were it not.

You wandered through earth's maze, as young folk do,
   Year in, year out, you hungered and were filled.
      You watched each turn for what was yours,
      And found your name, your face in book and news.
Yes, that was you . . . ,
                    but yet, you were it not.

You journeyed far; the sun descends behind you,
   Yet, one still goes before you, dark and long;
      Though most men you may overtake,
      This one keeps pace with you, and walks your gait.
That too, is you . . . ,
                    but yet, you are it not.

Do you then know, child of man, whom this describes . . . ?
   There stands a house: six boards make up its frame,
      Who dwells there is not asked his will;
      He lies there lonesome, lies there cold and still.
And that is you . . . ,
                    and yet, you are it not!

EXAMPLE FROM EAST PRUSSIA
The following poem was written in 1856 under the title "De ole Buerschmann em Warder an sine Fru" by Joh. O.L. August Lehman in his local dialect of Königsberg, East Prussia. In 1992, it was retitled and transcribed by Reuben Epp from its original Nether Prussian Low German dialect into Plautdietsch.

"De Bua aun siene Fru"	**"The Farmer to his Wife"**
Von Dr. Joh. O.L. August Lehman, 1856	A version in English
Königsberg, Ostpreußen	of Lehman's poem

Dit es een Dag soo wundascheen,
Aus ekj miendag nich hab jeseehn':
Du, truutste Fru, best schmock un fien,
Soo seet aus Zocka, koasch aus Wien.

Today's a day so beautiful,
Exceeding all that I have seen:
You, trusty wife, are fair and fine
As sweet as sugar, robust as wine.

Fer aule Leewe un Jeduld
Bliew ekj tiedläwens en dien Schuld;
Du pläagst soo trulich emma mi,
Woo kaun jenuag ekj danke di?

Your kindly love and sufferance
I cannot ever recompense;
You care for me so tenderly,
I know not what my thanks should be.

Boold steiht daut Metztje mi nich raicht,
De Kopp deit weeh, de Tiet es schlaicht,
Boold es't em Moage grausom fuul,
Boold lot ekj hänje Näs un Muul.

Then when my cap just won't sit straight,
My head just aches from soured fate,
My stomach ties itself in knots,
On nose and mouth hang dismal thoughts.

119

Du oba sorgst soo scheen fe' mi, Un wann ekj uk straumbolstrig si Un brommsch von miene Oabeit kom, Du hast mi daut nich schlaicht jenohm'.	Just then, you try to humor me, And though I may cantankerous be, And churlish from my work return, You never castigate nor spurn.

Du oba sorgst soo scheen fe' mi,
Un wann ekj uk straumbolstrig si
Un brommsch von miene Oabeit kom,
Du hast mi daut nich schlaicht jenohm'.

Du rädst mi emma frindlich too
Un moakst mien trurig Hoat soo frooh
Un semmeleascht met mi soo jeern,
Daut onse Kjinja goodet leahr'n.

D'rom dank ekj di ut Hoatens Grund;
Hool di mau straum, frooh un jesund;
De leewe Gott jäw Säajen di
Un onse Kjinjatjes un mi!

Just then, you try to humor me,
And though I may cantankerous be,
And churlish from my work return,
You never castigate nor spurn.

You're always friendly in your deed,
And cheer my heart when it's in need;
You gladly contemplate what we
Should teach our children, prudently.

For all, I thank you from my soul;
God keep you happy, sound and whole;
And may His blessings ever be
Upon our children, you and me!

Language and Dialect Comparisons
— Low German and English

The first two segments that follow are versions in two dialects of the opening paragraph of a story in "PLATTformen 91," published by STYX Publications of Groningen, Netherlands, 1991. "Zusters" by Hanny Diemer and "Süsters" by Johannes Diekhoff are in dialects of Groningen and East Friesland respectively. These excerpts from "PLATTformen 91" are reprinted with kind permission of STYX Publications. Other translations are as noted.

"Zusters" by Hanny Diemer, Groningen, Netherlands
"Binnen nait veul minsen doar k der mit over proat heb. t Zol ja kinnen dat ze mien verhoal nait leuven zollen of mie alderdeegs uutlaggen. Mor ie binnen der nou zo rusteg veur zitten goan, dat k heb t gevuil dat k joe t wel vertellen kin."

"Süsters" by Johannes Diekhoff, Aurich, East Friesland
"Dat gifft nich völ Minsken, mit de ik d'r over proot hebb. Ik reken, dat d'r nich völ Lü sünd, de mi mien Vertellsel glöven; utlachen sullen s' mi woll, as 'k meen. Man ji hebben jo dar nu so vull Andacht hensett, dat ik dat Geföhl hebb, dat ik jo 't woll vertellen dür."

"Süsters" by Günter Kühn, Oldenburg in Oldb., Germany
"Dat gifft nich vääl Minschen, mit de ik dar över snackt heff. Kann angahn, dat se mien Vertellsel garnich glöven of mi sogar utlachen schullen. Man Ji hebbt Jo dar so in Roh vörsett, dat ik't Geföhl heff, dat ik't Jo woll vertellen kann."

"Sestere" by Reuben Epp, in Mennonite Plautdietsch
"Et jefft woll nich väl Mensche met dän ekj doaräwa jerädt hab. Ekj meen, daut et nich väl Lied jefft dee mi mien Vetahlsel jleewe wudde;

120

utlache wudde se mi woll, jleew ekj. Oba nu daut Ji doa soo aundaichtig
sette, feehl ekj daut ekj et Ju vetahle kunn."

"Sisters" by Reuben Epp, in English
"There are not many people with whom I have spoken about this. I
think that many would not believe my story; most would laugh at me,
I suppose. But now that you are so attentatively seated here before me, I
have the feeling that I could tell it to you."

Summary of Chapter Eight

Changes in social attitudes engendered by the Industrial Revolution,
and the following Renaissance in Low German, promoted tolerance
toward the dialects in Germany, including Low German and the people
who spoke it. Modern enlightenment replaced the former ignorance of
Low German; benevolence and appreciation supplanted erstwhile negative attitudes. This change fostered increased literary activities among
the estimated eight million speakers of Low German, and a production
level of dialect literature unsurpassed by that of another language.
Universities and scholars increasingly recognized that the Low German
language was worthy of their attention.

Speakers of the Mennonite Plautdietsch dialect of Low German number an estimated three hundred thousand, and are scattered in various
countries of Europe and the Americas. But, their scholastic and literary
engagements in Low German do not yet approach the three to four percent of such activities that would be proportional to their numbers among
Low German people.

Among Plautdietsch Mennonites some express opinions that their Low
German mother tongue is inferior, that it cannot be written and that it
lacks culture. However, at least one scholar states that those who know
little about a language, have learned nothing of its history and have not
read its literature are not able to experience its achievements nor can
they appreciate its beauty.

A few self-motivated, literary-minded people have made themselves
known in written Plautdietsch. But, if it is to be written by more than
just a few, to meet or exceed its rightful and expected place in the Low
German literary world, it must receive more support from its people. This
can happen only when scholastic activities generate the enlightenment
needed to dispel existing misconceptions and the resulting negative perceptions and lack of appreciation.

The few examples of Low German literature quoted in this chapter
illustrate that Plautdietsch can indeed be written, and that it reflects
refinement and culture—when written by the refined and cultured
authors from whom they originated! These selected portions show that
speakers of Low German indeed can and should look up to this old mother tongue with pride.

Note: See Notes to Chapter One for Abbreviations.

1. *Die Gründunq des Instituts für niederdeutsche Sprache e.V.,* (Bremen: Institut fur niederdeutsche Sprache), p. 6.

2. Dieter Stellmacher, *Wer Spricht Platt?,* (Leer: Schuster Verlag Leer, 1987), p. 20.

3. John Holm, *Pidqins and Creoles.* Vol. 2, (Cambridge: Cambridge University Press, 1989). A recent letter from Barbara Grimes, Editor of Ethnologue, updates the figures for speakers of Plautdietsch for Belize to 7,440 with the assurance that the linguist Holm does accurate work.

4. This writer and other readers of this manuscript are of the opinion that the figures for speakers of Plautdietsch as first language and second language in Canada may have been erroneously reversed. Nevertheless, such opinions are unproven, therefore the figures are as quoted by Ethnologue.

5. Hans von Niessen, Geschäftsführer, Mennonitische Umsiedlerbetreuung, 5450 Neuwied, Langendorfer Straße 29,Germany, estimates approximately 35,000 to 40,000 people of Mennonite ancestry remain in the CIS (former USSR), and that 50% or more of them speak Plautdietsch, hence 17,500 to 20,000 speakers of Plautdietsch .

6. Prof. Dr. Irmtraud Rösler, University of Rostock, responds in November 1992 to a request for information on the number of speakers of Low German in the former East Germany by informing that such information is not available because a necessary survey has not been done. She further informs that results deriving from such a survey recently undertaken jointly by the universities of Kiel and Greifswald are expected to become available in1994.

7. Barbara Grimes, Editor of Ethnologue, informs in December 1992 that it is a mistake to assume that the proportions of speakers of Low German in East and West Germany are the same. The proportion in East Germany may be lower. Authoritative figures as noted in the foregoing note are not expected to be available until 1994.

8. Hans von Niessen, Mennonitische Umsiedlerbetreuung, states that their records show that more than 75,000 people of Mennonite extraction have come to Germany as immigrants from the former USSR. He does not include years or dates, but it can be assumed that the majority have arrived in the last decades (during the era of Glasnost and Perestroika) up to August 1992, when these figures were provided. He estimates that another 20,000 have arrived in Germany without registering with Umsiedlerbetreuung, and therefore do not appear on their records. This brings the total to 95,000 persons, which he conservatively places at 90,000, of whom he estimates that 60,000 speak Mennonite Plautdietsch. Hence, the estimated figure.

9. The estimated figure of 25% of the population (who speak Low Saxon) in these three provinces of the Netherlands: Groningen, Drenthe and Overijssel, has been corroborated by local (Kelowna, B.C.) former residents of the Netherlands. They agree that the estimate of 25% is modest and realistic.

10. Population figures for the provinces of the Netherlands are from *Encyclopædia Britannica,* 1991.

11. *Quickborn. Zeitschrift fur plattdeutsche Sprache und Dichtung,* 82. Jahrgang, 1992, No.1, (Hamburg: Vereinigung Quickborn in Hamburg, 1992) p. 83. According to an article which first appeared in the Kansas City Star, 1991, the small town of Cole Camp, Missouri, USA, staged a Low German Theatre on the 12th and 13th of October 1991 . It is said that a dialect of Low German is still well preserved among its people. It is not Mennonite Plautdietsch. The article intimates that the speakers are Lutherans.

12. Wolfgang Lindow und Claus Schuppenhauer, *Plattdeutsch im Buchhandel. 6. Auflage. 1991,* (Bremen: Institut fur niederdeutsche Sprache, 1991).

13. Ernst Christ of Radio NDR for Schleswig-Holstein, located in Kiel, Germany, responded most courteously with the included radio programming listings in answer to my request of July 1992 for information on their broadcasting of Low German language programming.

14. Seminar für Deutsche Philologie, der Georg-August-Universität Göttingen, Herr Prof. Dr. Dieter Stellmacher, Humboldtallee 13, 3400 Göttingen, Germany.

15. Universität Hamburg, Germanisches Seminar, Herr Prof. Dr. Dieter Möhn, Von-Melle-Park 6, 2000 Hamburg 13, Germany.

16. Universität Kiel, Germanistisches Seminar, Herr Prof. Dr. Hubertus Menke, Olshausenstraße 40-60.
—Herr Dr. Ulrich Tolksdorf, Leiter: Preußisches Wörterbuch, Neue Universitat, Haus N 50c, Olshausenstraße 40/60, 2300 Kiel 1, Germany.

17. Universität Münster, Herr Prof. Dr. Jan Goossens, Magdalenenstraße 5, 440 Munster, Germany

18. Prof. Dr. Hermann Niebaum, Vakgroep Taalwetenschap, Rijksuniversiteit Groningen, Oude Kijk in't Jatstraat 26, Postbus 716, 9700 AS Groningen, Netherlands.

19. Prof. Dr. Tjeerd de Graaf, Vakgroep Taalwetenschap, Rijksuniversiteit Groningen, Oude Kijk in't Jatstraat 26, Postbus 716, 9700 AS Groningen, Netherlands.

20. Dieter Möhn, "Geschichte der niederdeutschen Mundarten," *NSL*, 1983, pp. 163-164.

21. Harry Loewen and Al Reimer, "Origins and Literary Development of Canadian-Mennonite Low German." *MQR*, (Goshen: Mennonite Historical Society, Goshen College, Goshen, Indiana, Volume LIX, Number 3, July 1985), pp. 279-286.

22. Unruh, pp. 12, 16.

23. W.W. Moelleken, "Die Rußlanddeutschen Mennoniten in Kanada und Mexico," *Zeitschrift für Dialektoloaie und Linauistik. LIV. Jahrgang*, Heft 2, 1987. p. 169.

24. Dieter Stellmacher, *Wer Spricht Platt?*, (Bremen: Institut für niederdeutsche Sprache, 1987), p. 43. Stellmacher says, "Daß das Niederdeutsche von denen gering geschätzt wird, die von ihm wenig wissen, uberrrascht nicht." (That Low German is held in low esteem by those who know little about it, is not surprising).

25. Unruh, p. 33.

26. Dieter Stellmacher, *Wer Spricht Platt?*, p. 43.

27. Johann Dietrich Bellmann, "Niederdeutsch als Kirchensprache," *NSL*, p. 617-618.

28. W. Ziesemer, *Die Ostpreußischen Mundarten*, (Wiesbaden: Dr. Martin Sandig oHG., 1970 [Neudruck der Ausgabe 1924]), p. 111.

29. Stellmacher, *Wer Spricht Platt?*, p. 43.

30. Jorg Eiben-von Hertell, "Lyrik," *NSL*, p. 419.

31. Dieter Stellmacher, *Niederdeutsche Sprache*, (Bern: Verlag Peter Lang AG, 1990), p. 197.

32. Gerhard Hinsch, "Schreibung des Niederdeutschen," *NSL*, pp. 202-203.

33. Horst Penner, p. 180.

34. Tjeerd de Graaf, "Op bezoek bij de Mennonieten, in Siberië spreken ze Grunnings," (Groningen: *Trojka Magazine*, March 1992), p. 4.

BIBLIOGRAPHY

Dictionaries (Titles):

German-English Dictionary (A New), F.C. Hebert and L. Hirsch, (Philadelphia: David Mckay Company, 19??)

German-English Dictionary (Concise), Langenscheidt's, (London: Hodder and Stoughton Limited, 1973)

Große Duden (Der), Dudenredaktion, (Mannheim: Bibliographisches Institut AG, 1961)

Kjenn Jie noch Plautdietsch?, [A Mennonite Low German Dictionary], Herman Rempel, (Winnipeg: Mennonite Literary Society, 1984). pp.295.

Mennonite Low German Dictionary, [Mennonitisches Wörterbuch], Jack Thiessen, (Marburg: N.G. Elwert Verlag, 1977) pp.70.

Oxford Dictionary of English Etymology (The), C.T. Onions, (New York and Oxford: Oxford University Press, 1966)

Plattdeutsches Wörterbuch, Hermann Böning, (Dinklage: Verlag Heimatverein Herrlichkeit, 1970)

Plattdeutsches Wörterbuch, Wolfgang Lindow, (Bremen: Institut für niederdeutsche Sprache, 1984)

Preußisches Wörterbuch, Hermann Frischbier, [Nachdruck der Ausgabe Berlin, 1882] (Hildesheim.New York: Georg Olms Verlag, 1971)

Preußisches Wörterbuch, Erhard Riemann u. Ulrich Tolksdorf, (Neumünster: Karl Wachholtz Verlag, 1974-1992, [fi - Rutzen]

So schabberten wir to Hus, Rudolf K. Becker,(Leer, Ostfriesland: Verlag Gerhard Rautenberg, 1975)

Webster's Encyclopedic Unabridged Dictionary, (New York: Gramercy Books, 1989)

Reference Texts (Titles):

Atlas zur deutschen Sprache (dtv-), Werner König, (München: Deutscher Taschenbuch Verlag, 1978)

Encyclopædia Britannica, (Chicago: William Benton, Publisher, 1959) and (Chicago: Encyclopædia Britannica Inc., 15th Edit., 1990)

Handbuch zur niederdeutschen Sprach- und Literaturwissenschaft, NSL, Gerhard Cordes und Dieter Möhn, (Berlin: Erich Schmidt Verlag GmbH, 1983)

Mennonite Encyclopedia, (Scottdale, Pennsylvania: The Mennonite Publishing House, 1955, 1969)

Mennonite Historical Atlas, William Schroeder and Helmut Huebert, (Winnipeg: Springfield Publishers, 1990), pp. 132.

World Book Atlas, World Book Encyclopedia, Inc., (Chicago: Rand McNally & Company, 1980)

Reference Texts (Authors):

Claiborne, Robert, *Our Marvelous Native Tongue,* (New York: Times Books,1983)

Friesen, P.M., *The Mennonite Brotherhood in Russia 1789-1910,* [2. Revised Edition 1980], (Board of Christian Literature, General Conference of Mennonite Brethren Churches, 1980)

Klassen, Peter J., *A Homeland for Strangers,* (Fresno, California: Center for Mennonite Brethren Studies, 1989)

McCrum, Robert, William Cran and Robert McNeil, *The Story of English,* (New York: Elisabeth Sifton Books - Viking Penguin Inc. 1986)

Penner, Horst, *Weltweite Bruderschaft,* [4. Auflage überarbeitet von Horst Gerlach und Horst Quiring], (Weierhof: Verlag mennonitischer Geschichtsverein, 1984)

Schuppenhauer, Claus, *Niederdeutsch Heute,* (Bremen: Institut für niederdeutsche Sprache, 1976)

Smith, Henry C., *The Story of the Mennonites,* [fourth Edition], (Newton Kansas: Mennonite Publication Office, 1957)

Stellmacher, Dieter, *Niederdeutsch,* [Formen und Forschungen], Reihe germanistische Linguistik, (Tübingen: Max Niemeyer Verlag, 1981)

— *Niederdeutsche Sprache,* [Langs Germanistische Lehrbuchsammlung, Band 26], (Bern: Verlag Peter Lang AG, 1990)

— *Wer Spricht Platt?,* (Bremen: Institut für niederdeutsche Sprache, 1987)

Stumpp, Karl, *Die Auswanderung aus Deutschland nach Rußland in den Jahren 1763-1862,* (Landmannschaft der Deutschen aus Rußland, 1991) [5. Auflage]

Urry, James, *None But Saints,* (Hyperion Press Limited, 1989)

Ziesemer, Walther, *Ostpreußischen Mundarten (Die),* [Neudruck der Ausgabe 1924], (Wiesbaden: Dr. Martin Sändig oHG, 1970)

Dissertations and Research Papers (Authors):

Buchheit, Robert H., *Mennonite "Plautdietsch":* A phonological and morphological description of a settlement dialect in York and Hamilton Counties, Nebraska, [A Dissertation], (Lincoln: University of Nebraska, 1978)

Dyck, Henry Dietrich, *Language Differentiation in two Low German Groups in Canada,* [A Dissertation], (University of Pennsylvania, 1964)

Penner, Horst, *Die Ost- und westpreußischen Mennoniten:* in ihrem religiösen und sozialen Leben, in ihren kulturellen und wirtschaftlichen Leistungen, Teil I, 1526 bis 1772, (Weierhof: Mennonitischer Geschichtsverein E.V., 1978)

Quiring, Jacob (Walter), *Die Mundart von Chortitza in Süd-Rußland,*
[Inaugural Dissertation], (München: Druckerei Studentenhaus,
1928)
Rijksuniversiteit Groningen, *De taal der Mennonieten,* Groningen,
Netherlands, 1992. A report on a symposium on Plautdietsch
held 24 October 1992. 42 pp.
Unruh, Benjamin Heinrich, *Die Niederländisch-niederdeutsche
Hintergründe der mennonitischen Ostwanderungen im 16., 18.
und 19. Jahrhundert,* (Karlsruhe: Im Selbstverlag, 1955)
Urry, James, "From Speech to Literature," Low German and
Mennonite Identity in Two Worlds. *History and Anthropology,*
1991, Vol. 5, No. 2, pp. 233-258. (Victoria University of
Wellington, New Zealand, 1991)
Wicherkiewicz, Tomasz, *Sporen van de Mennonieten in Noord-Polen,*
(Poznań, Poland: Adam Mickiewicz-Universiteit, 1992) 5 pp.
Zhirmunskii, Viktor Maksimovich, *Dialectical and Ethnographical
Studies of German Settlements in the USSR,* (A Summary of and
Problems relating to). First published 1933 in Russian.

Journals, Periodicals and other publications (Titles):

Bericht, Bevensen Tagung, Jahrestagung für Niederdeutsch,(Bevensen: Im
Auftrage des Vorstandes der Bevensen-Tagunge.V.)
Gründung des Instituts für niederdeutsche Sprache e.V., Stellung
und Aufgaben des Instituts, (Bremen: vom Gründungsbeirat, 1973)
Journal of Mennonite Studies, JMS, (Winnipeg: University of
Winnipeg)
Mennonite Life, (North Newton, Kansas: Bethel College)
Mennonite Quarterly Review (The), MQR, (Goshen: the Mennonite
Historical Society for Goshen College and the Associated
Mennonite Biblical Seminaries)
Plattdeutsch im Buchhandel, PIB, Lindow und Schuppenhauer,
(Bremen: Institut für niederdeutsche Sprache)
Plattdeutsche Bibliographie, Friedrich W. Michelson, (Bremen:
Institut für niederdeutsche Sprache)
Quickborn, Zeitschrift für plattdeutsche Sprache und Dichtung,
(Hamburg: Vereinigung Quickborn)
PLATTformen 91, Streektaalliteratur uut Groningen, Drenthe, het
Emsland en Oostfriesland (Groningen: STYX Publications, 1991)
Westpreußen-Jahrbuch, (Münster [Westf.]: Westpreußen Verlag, 1991)
Zeitschrift für Dialektologie und Linguistik, (Sitz Stuttgart: Franz
Steiner Verlag Wiesbaden GmbH)

Relevant Books (Authors):

Dyck, Arnold, *Works of Arnold Dyck (Collected),* (Vols. II and III),
Edited by Al Reimer, (Winnipeg: Manitoba Mennonite Historical
Society, 1986,1988)

127

Epp, Frank H., *Mennonite Exodus*, (Altona, Manitoba: Canadian
Mennonite Relief and Immigration Council, 1962)
Fissen, Karl, *Plattdütsch Läwt!*, (Oldenburg: Heinz Holzberg Verlag, 1963)
Nimtz-Wendland, Wanda, *Erzählgut der Kurischen Nehrung*, (Marburg:
N.G. Elwert Verlag, 1961)
Rosenburg, Siegried, *Geschichte des Kreises Großes Werder*,
(Klausdorf/Schwentine: Danziger Verlagsgesellschaft Paul
Rosenburg, 1939?)
Specht, Fritz, *Plattdeutsch wie es nicht im Wörterbuch steht*,
(Frankfurt am Main: Verlag Heinrich Scheffler, 1969)
Thiessen, Jack and Victor Peters, *Plautdietsche Jeschichten*,
(Marburg: N.G. Elwert Verlag, 1990)
Tolksdorf, Ulrich, *Eine ostpreußische Volkserzählerin*, (Marburg:
N.G. Elwert Verlag, 1980)

Articles (Authors)

Bender, Harold S., "Language Problems," *Mennonite Encyclopedia*,
(Scottdale: The Mennonite Publishing House, 1969) pp. 290-292.
Cordes, Gerhard, "Altniederdeutsche Grammatik," *NSL*, pp. 206-208.
— "Geschichte und Methoden der niederdeutschen Literatur-
wissenschaft," *NSL*, pp. 24-68.
— "Mittelniederdeutsche Dichtung und Gebrauchsliteratur,"
NSL, pp. 351-390.
— "Mittelniederdeutsche Grammatik," *NSL*, pp. 209-237.
Dal, Ingerid, "Altniederdeutsch und seine Vorstufen," *NSL*, pp. 69-97.
de Graaf, Tjeerd, "Language of the Siberian Mennonites," A study
at the University of Groningen, Netherlands. (Vakgroep
Taalwetenschap, Faculteit der Letteren: Ronde 1992) pp. 1-9.
— "Op bezoek bij de Mennonieten, In Siberië spreken ze
Grunnings," *Trojka Magazine*, March 1992, (Groningen: Gremi
Auto Import bv)
— "Tippeltoan, zo hait dij hoan, wiedewiedewoan,"
Gronings nog steeds springlevend bij Mennonieten in
Novosibirsk, *De Streek*, Drenta, Groningse, Pers, Vrijdag
13 december 1991.
Epp, Reuben, "Low German: Where it came from; and where it's
going," *Mennonite Mirror*, January 1989, pp. 5-6.
— "Plautdietsch: Language or Dialect?" *Mennonite Mirror*,
May 1986, pp. 19-21.
— "Plautdietsch: Origins, Development and State of the Low
German Language," *JMS*, 1987, pp. 60-72.
Gabrielsson, Artur, "Verdrängung der mittelniederdeutschen durch
die neuhochdeutsche Schriftsprache," *NSL*, pp. 119-153.
Gerlach, Horst, "Von Westpreußen nach Rußland," Hintergründe und
Bedeutung der mennonitischen Auswanderung, *Westpreußen
Jahrbuch*, Bd. 41, (Münster: Westpreußen Verlag, 1991) 98-114.

Gerlach, Horst, "Die Wehrfreiheit der ost- und westpreußischen Mennoniten und die Reichsversammlung von 1848," *Westpreußen Jahrbuch,* Bd.24, (Münster: Landmannschaft Westpreußen, 1974)   pp. 110-115.

Huber, Wolfgang, "Altniederdeutsche Dichtung," *NSL,* pp. 334-350.

Hyldgaard-Jensen, Karl, "Mittelniederdeutsch und die skandinavischen Sprachen," *NSL,* pp. 666-677.

Loewen, Harry, "The German-Russian Tensions among the Mennonites in Russia, 1789-1917, *P.M. Friesen and his History,* (Fresno, California: Center for Mennonite Brethren Studies, 1979), pp. 133-152.

Loewen, Harry and Al Reimer, "Origins and Literary Development of Canadian-Mennonite Low German," *MQR,* July 1985, pp. 279-286.

Moelleken, W.W., "Die Linguistische Heimat der Russlanddeutschen Mennoniten in Kanada und Mexico," *Jahrbuch des Vereins für niederdeutsche Sprachforschung,* (Neumünster: Karl Wachholtz Verlag, 1987) pp. 89-123.

— "Die Rußlanddeutschen Mennoniten in Kanada und Mexiko: sprachliche Entwicklung und diglossische Situation," *Zeitschrift für Dialektologie,* LIV. Jahrgang, Heft 2, 1987, (Sitz Stuttgart: Franz Steiner Verlag Wiesbaden GmbH) pp. 145-183

— "Spracherhaltungsfaktoren in den mexikanischen Siedlungen der rußlandeutschen Mennoniten," aus *Germanistische Mitteilungen* 24/1986, pp. 61-81.

Möhn, Dieter, "Geschichte der neuniederdeutschen Mundarten," *NSL,* pp. 154-181.

Moss, Christopher, "Niederdeutsch-englische Zusammenhänge," *NSL,* pp. 660-665.

Rempel, David G., "Mennonite Commonwealth in Russia (The): A sketch of its founding and endurance, 1789-1919," *MQR,* October 1973,   pp. 259-308, and January 1974, pp. 05-54.

Stellmacher, Dieter, "Neuniederdeutsche Grammatik," *NSL,* pp. 238-278.

Thiessen, Jack, "Arnold Dyck — the Mennonite Artist," *Mennonite Life,* April 1969, (Newton, Kansas: Bethel College), pp. 77-83.

— "Canadian Mennonite Literature," Canadian Literature Quarterly, U.B.C., Editor - George Woodcock, 1972, pp. 65-72.

— "Deutschunterricht in den Prärieprovinzen," *Deutsch als Muttersprache in Kanada,* Bd.1, (Mannheim: Institut für deutsche Sprache, 1977, pp. 93-96.

— "Dietsche Jasch," Ein Indianer aus dem Chaco erzählt in plattdeutscher Mundart, *Jahrbuch für ostdeutsche Volkskunde,* Bd.27, (Marburg: N:G: Elwert Verlag, 1984) pp. 326-332.

— "Low German of the Canadian Mennonites," *Mennonite Life,*

July 1967, (Newton, Kansas: Bethel College) pp. 110-116

— "Low German (Plautdietsch) in Manitoba," *German-Canadian Yearbook,* (Toronto: Historical Society of Mecklenburg Upper Canada, 1986), pp. 127-137.

— "Mennoniten Plautdietsch, Woher? Wohin?" *Der Bote,* 1. April, 1992, (Winnipeg: Allgemeine Konferenz der Mennoniten in Kanada) p. 4.

— "A New Look at an old Problem:" Origins of the Variations in Mennonite Plautdietsch, *MQR,* July 1988, pp. 285-296

— "Sprichwörter im Niederdeutsch der kanadischen Mennoniten," *Jahrbuch des Vereins für niederdeutsche Sprachforschung,* (Neumünster: Karl Wachholtz Verlag, 1968) pp. 109-120.

— "Zur Frage der Identität der Mennoniten," *Jahrbuch für ostdeutsche Volkskunde,* Bd.33, (Marburg: N:G: Elwert Verlag, 1990), pp. 439-447.

Tolksdorf, Ulrich, "Die Mundarten Danzigs und seines Umlandes," *Danzig in acht Jahrhunderten,* (Münster: Nicolaus-Copernicus-Verlag, 1985) pp. 313-336.

— "Die Mundartliteratur Westpreußens," *Westpreußen Jahrbuch,* Bd.42, (Münster: Westpreußen Verlag, 1992) pp. 65-82

— "Niederdeutsche Gelegenheitsgedichte des 18. Jahrhunderts aus Danzig und Elbing," *Jahrbuch für ostdeutsche Volkskunde,* Bd.29, (Marburg: N:G: Elwert Verlag, 1986) pp. 218-232.

Urry, James, "The Russian State, the Mennonite World and the Migration from Russia to North America in the 1870's," *Mennonite Life,* p. 12.

* **Dr. David G. Rempel,** among his many works on the history of the Mennonites, wrote "The Mennonite Commonwealth in Russia — A Sketch of its founding and Endurance, 1789-1919," which appeared in the Mennonite Quarterly Review for October 1973 and January 1974. Its review of Mennonite history in Russia provided much information relevant to this "Story of Low German — and Plautdietsch." It is repeatedly referred to in the notes. David Rempel died in Menlo Park, California on 27th June, 1992, at the age of 92.

** **Dr. Ulrich Tolksdorf** was the Editor of "Preußisches Würterbuch" and the author of numerous scholarly works on various facets of Low German and language in Prussia, including Mennonite Plautdietsch. His published works provide much factual information for this "Story" and are frequently referred to in the notes. Shortly before his death, he began working on an "Akustisches Wörterbuch" (Audio Dictionary) of Mennonite Low German. Ulrich Tolksdorf died on the 9th of September 1992 at the age of 54 years while in the employ of the University of Kiel.

Index